Praise for **Bridging the Boomer-Xer Gap**

"This book provides a much-needed breakthrough in management's quest to overcome the chasm of discontent between generations in our organizations. Employers of Choice know that they must solve generational differences in communication style and work approach. The research and insights in *Bridging the Boomer-Xer Gap* explain a new concept—authentic teams that value individuality—and provide a road map for managers to solve Gen X recruiting and retention issues."

NANCY S. AHLRICHS, SPHR, AUTHOR, *COMPETING FOR TALENT*

"This book shatters the Boomers' prevailing stereotypes about Gen Xers' work habits and values. It will help you understand and appreciate your Xers, create 'authentic teams' to bridge the generation gap among employees, and improve productivity, loyalty, and innovation in your business."

BARBARA WEAVER SMITH, PRESIDENT,
SMITH WEAVER SMITH "CULTURAL CHANGEMAKERS"

"We have all heard the hyperbole about generation gaps. The two refreshing contributions of this book are data that document the real differences—not just hyped opinions—and concrete and helpful suggestions for appropriate action."

W. WARNER BURKE, PROFESSOR OF PSYCHOLOGY AND EDUCATION,
TEACHERS COLLEGE, COLUMBIA UNIVERSITY

BRIDGING THE
BOOMER
XER GAP

BRIDGING THE
BOOMER XER GAP

CREATING AUTHENTIC TEAMS FOR HIGH PERFORMANCE AT WORK

HANK KARP   CONNIE FULLER   DANILO SIRIAS

DAVIES-BLACK PUBLISHING
PALO ALTO, CALIFORNIA

THIS BOOK is dedicated to those who taught us to appreciate the nuances of organizational life, pioneers in the study of organizational behavior, Gestalt theory, and OD. It is also dedicated to the Boomers in our own lives, our family and friends, and to the Xers, our children and their friends, who help us daily to see the world in a whole new way. Thank you.

Published by Davies-Black Publishing, an imprint of Consulting Psychologists Press, Inc., 3803 East Bayshore Road, Palo Alto, CA 94303; 800-624-1765.

Special discounts on bulk quantities of Davies-Black books are available to corporations, professional associations, and other organizations. For details, contact the Director of Book Sales at Davies-Black Publishing, an imprint of Consulting Psychologists Press, Inc., 3803 East Bayshore Road, Palo Alto, CA 94303; 650-691-9123; fax 650-623-9271.

Visit the Davies-Black Publishing web site at www.daviesblack.com.

06 05 04 03 02   10 9 8 7 6 5 4 3 2 1

Printed in the United States of America

Library of Congress Cataloging-in-Publication Data

Karp, Hank
    Bridging the boomer-xer gap : creating authentic teams for high perfor-mance at work / Hank Karp, Connie Fuller, Danilo Sirias.
       p. cm.
    Includes bibliographical references and index.

    ISBN 0-89106-159-2

    1. Teams in the workplace. 2. Conflict of generations. 3. Generation X.

    4. Baby boom generation. I. Fuller, Connie II. Sirias, Danilo III. Title.

    HD66 . K374 2001
    658.4'02 — dc21

                    2001047052

FIRST EDITION
First printing 2002

Contents

Foreword

One of the first things that endeared this book, *Bridging the Boomer-Xer Gap*, to me I found in its Introduction. When the authors say, "... findings were surprising to us. They were just opposite of our expectation," I, for one, take notice. For me, the best models (and research) show where to look. They do not tell me what to see. *Bridging the Boomer-Xer Gap* points to several places that are well worth the looking.

This book's most important theme is its emphasis on the importance of authenticity for teams, whether those teams are composed of Gen Xers or Baby Boomers or both. It is certainly a relevant theme for today, as well as for the future. In this age of networked organizations, what some have called the "New Economy," there is a rapidly expanding use of teams of all kinds.

Teams are increasingly important in the workplace, and this requires a fundamental reexamination of the ways we work with others, both collectively and as individuals. In one example, Carol Willett of Applied Knowledge Group, Inc., has, with her colleagues, spent nearly thirty years forming and leading globally dispersed virtual teams with many members who never have face-to-face contact with their co-workers. She says, "Some managers seem to think that going to virtual teams involves little more than connecting computers and loading the groupware. Some are also relieved by their assumption that the electronic interchange pretty much eliminates the messy people problems they used to have to deal with. They are likely to be disappointed. There is more to team effectiveness than the mechanics."

The complexity to which Willett refers is that we still have to concentrate on the human-to-human interface. One of the most commonly heard complaints of team members is that it takes too much time and too much work to come to a consensus-based decision among a large group of people with diverse backgrounds and self-interests. Another is that consensus decisions, when they are made, are often compromises that lack boldness and imaginative power. These issues are among the challenges of effective teams that this book helps to address.

Most team issues fall into three categories:

- Group cohesion and morale building

- Establishing individual identity

- Assuring interaction processes that contribute to effective performance

If a team is to be successful, it is clear that considerable attention must be exercised by its members in consideration of others' thoughts and feelings. But what happens when politeness and politics become the highest priority? Does that outlaw spontaneity and obscure substantive argument to the detriment of clarity and the possibilities of creative controversy? The authors address these kinds of issues for the team that contains different generations. The guidelines provided for building authentic teams are not only helpful for self-managed teams; they provide clues for other types of work teams as well.

Among the valuable guides you will find in this book that will be particularly useful to managers, as well as to those responsible for recruiting and training, is chapter 7's comparisons and suggestions for retaining employees. *Bridging the Boomer-Xer Gap* will provide you with a framework you can use in achieving a sharper focus for dealing with both Gen Xers and Baby Boomers—indeed, for dealing with all people in more direct, effective, and personally satisfying ways.

Stan Herman
Author of *A Force of Ones* and *The Tao at Work*

Acknowledgments

This book is about the men and women of all ages who make our organizations strong, whose individual energy and creativity allow us to survive the continuous and unrelenting change that characterizes the twenty-first-century world of work. The fact that each man and each woman is uniquely different from the other should be a cause for great celebration. Unfortunately, all too often it is just the opposite. We use the yardstick of our own behavior to pass judgment on those around us, and to offer criticism rather than praise when we find differences. If we stop to imagine a world in which we are all alike, however, we quickly realize that such a world would be pretty boring, and unlikely to survive for very long. It is our differences that give us strength and vitality, that provide challenges and options. It is our differences that keep things interesting and give us an opportunity to learn and grow.

We did not set out with the intent of writing a book that needed to be written. Rather, a book that needed to be written found us. What eventually emerged from our initial questions about the working relationship between Boomers and Xers surprised us, and then delighted us. Through the lens of possibilities, tempered by real-life experiences, we came to see a vision of the future that was subtly but critically different from what had been envisioned by others. This book is our road map for making that vision a reality. It's a simple road map, but not an easy one. Following the path we have laid before you in this book requires you to set aside some long-held assumptions and the behaviors that go with them. It offers, in return, an opportunity to create a future that celebrates the best in each of us.

We want to take this opportunity to thank the many people at Davies-Black Publishing who helped us bring this book to completion. We are grateful to Melinda Adams Merino, our first editor, who challenged us to take on this task. We owe many thanks to Alan Shrader, the editor who guided us through the sometimes painful evolution of the manuscript. And to Connie Kallback, whose excitement about the book breathed life into the final product, thank you for giving us the energy and the confidence to make it to the finish line. To Laura Simonds and Jill Anderson-Wilson, who brought us reality in the form of marketing and production plans, thank you for proving to us that this book was, in fact, going to happen. And to the many other people at Davies-Black whose names we do not know but whose efforts we appreciate more than we can say, thank you.

We would also like to express our thanks to Meredith Hines, our research assistant on the first study, and to Tanya Christopher, our research assistant on the second. The unsung heroes or, in this case, heroines of any research project are those who have to slog through the raw data, enter it, and make it understandable before the researchers even look at it. Ladies, our deepest gratitude. We couldn't have done it without you.

Finally, we want to thank our families and friends, who were always patient with our book-related distractions and forever interested in our progress. We are especially excited to be sharing this accomplishment with you.

About the Authors

H. B. (HANK) KARP, PH.D.

Hank Karp received his Ph.D. degree in industrial and organizational psychology from Case Western Reserve University, Cleveland, Ohio, in 1969. He completed his postdoctoral work in Gestalt therapy through the Intensive Postgraduate Program at the Gestalt Institute of Cleveland in 1974. In addition, he is a licensed Professional Counselor in Virginia.

After leaving the academic setting, where he was a tenured associate professor on Old Dominion University's faculty of management for ten years, Karp organized his own consulting firm, Personal Growth Systems, in 1979. His specialties include management training and development, organization development, and executive coaching. Karp is currently on the faculty of management at Christopher Newport University in Newport News, Virginia.

Clients in the corporate sector have included American Can Company, Pepsi-Cola Company, General Dynamics, IBM, Chaparral Steel Company, Miles Laboratories Corporation, FMC Marine Colloids, Hoechst Celanese Corporation, and Reads Ltd. (England). In the human services sector, Karp has worked with the City of Virginia Beach, Norfolk Social Services, the Virginia Department of Corrections, the U.S. Navy, the Federal Aviation Administration, the Smithsonian Institution, and many other agencies at local, state, and federal levels.

He has designed public seminars for managers in the areas of first-line leadership skill development; power; conflict and resistance; delegation; motivation and job enrichment; leadership style and managerial effectiveness; Gestalt organization development; and career plateauing. These seminars have been conducted through university management centers throughout the United States and Canada, including UCLA, SMU, University of Pittsburgh, William & Mary, Temple University, and McGill University. Karp has conducted public seminars in first-line supervision for Penton Learning Systems, the American Management Association, and other sponsoring organizations. He has also conducted many weekend personal growth workshops for individuals.

Author of two books, *The Change Leader: Using a Gestalt Approach with Work Groups* (1996) and *Personal Power: An Unorthodox Guide to*

Success (1995), Karp has also published many articles. His professional memberships include the American Psychological Association, the OD Network, and the Gestalt Institute of Cleveland.

CONNIE FULLER
Connie Fuller is an Organization Development Specialist with AG Communication Systems, a subsidiary of Lucent Technologies. She has worked in organization development for nearly twenty years, with a focus on self-directed work teams for the past eight years. In addition to her corporate work, Fuller teaches courses in organization development, organizational behavior, and management for Webster University. She is currently completing doctoral work in organization development at Benedictine University in Lisle, Illinois.

DANILO SIRIAS
Danilo Sirias holds a master's degree in industrial and systems engineering and a Ph.D. degree in production and operations management, both from the University of Memphis. He is also a certified academic in the Theory of Constraints and currently is a faculty member in the Department of Management and Marketing at Christopher Newport University in Newport News, Virginia. Sirias has conducted research presentations at national and international conferences. His research includes applications of Theory of Constraints to different business issues, including teamwork. He has received several grants and awards, including an Outstanding Paper Award for "creative use of scientific inquiry" from the Sigma Xi Scientific Research Society.

Introduction

We would like to tell you a little bit about how this book got started, where it came from, and where we think it is going. The first part of the book deals with background. It addresses the existing conditions between Baby Boomers and Generation X employees in the workplace. The research described in chapter 2 was designed to explore these generational conditions. The research findings were surprising to us. They were just opposite of our expectations, and they opened the door to a whole new realm of possibilities, both positive and negative, for the mix of generations that will make up the workforce for decades to come.

One company that participated in the original research stood out. In that team-based organization, the differences between Baby Boomers and Generation X employees virtually disappeared. For people in certain work teams, workplace values and behaviors were in sync regardless of age differences between the team members. A closer look at conditions that might explain this difference proved worthwhile. What we learned from our investigation of those teams led us to the insights we write about in this book. Beginning with chapter 3, we talk about how the findings of the research directed us to a workplace design that is similar to, yet significantly different from, what happens in most organizations today.

Our suggestions and implementation recommendations, which form the remainder of the book, are not rocket science. But they point to an important refinement of what has been common knowledge to date. We have put a significant new twist on teamwork and team development that will bring meaningful rewards to the organizations and employees who put our recommendations into practice.

You may be tempted to go directly to findings and recommendations, ignoring the background and research described in the early chapters of the book. In today's time-pressed environment, that's what we tend to do in order to survive. However, we ask that you make this book an exception and read it from start to finish. Reading the last chapter of a mystery novel before reading the rest tells you what happened, but you still don't know why. Reading the book from start to finish allows you to fit our framework into your experiences and the needs of your situation.

Many options are offered, and there will be some that are right for you and some that aren't. You will know which is which only if you are firmly grounded in what the options are designed to accomplish. We think you will be "hooked" by the possibilities, just as we were as the research unfolded before us. A similar adventure awaits you as you look at your own organization and the possibilities it holds.

The first segment of the workforce considered in this book is the generation known as Baby Boomers. Born between 1945 and 1962, Boomers are today coming into control of their organizations. They are filling the ranks of management and putting their own thumbprint on how organizations are run. Team-based learning, participative decision making, and shared reward systems are all facets of Boomer management ideals. Boomers have been waiting for years to undo the autocracy of the past and move into an enlightened and harmonious future.

The second segment of today's workforce is the generation known as Generation Xers, those born between 1963 and 1982, of whom well over 40 million are gainfully employed. Gen Xers bring to the workforce values, education, and experiences that are quite different from those of their parents. Xers are high-tech, independent individuals who will leave one job for another that is more interesting or simply to have more time for personal pursuits or time to spend with friends. Boomers are horrified at the perceived lack of loyalty and lack of responsibility exhibited by their Gen X co-workers, and Xers are continually reminding their older fellow workers to "chill out."

This scenario sets up some obvious differences in views between the two but begs the question "Is there really a qualitative difference in values and outlook between Baby Boomers and Generation Xers?" We know that each generation is somewhat different from its predecessor. Yet, in a society that is not currently experiencing great social or political upheaval, change and development are more often evolutionary than revolutionary. Some differences always occur between generations, if for no other reason than that the younger generation wants to assert its independence from the older one. Looking briefly back at the past half century, each decade has had its sobriquet. The fifties produced the "Beat Generation," and the sixties the "hippies." In the seventies, it was the "Me Generation," and in the eighties the yuppies. Now we have "Generation X," the generation of the nineties. Whether we talk about discrete decades or fifteen-to-twenty-year generational periods, surface attributes observably change, and the core issues that define each group seem dissimilar. Yet, each outgoing generation leaves only a small measure of permanent change behind. Thus, the overall culture changes slowly, and the cultural metamorphosis is ongoing. Under this traditional scenario, Generation X is just the next group to be identified as a step along the path of progression, with little of real substance separating it from the generation before it.

There is another view, however. Due to recent rapid changes in Western civilization related to both social conditions and advancing technology, Generation X is growing up under a set of societal conditions that is significantly different from any known before. A qualitative difference exists in how Generation Xers view the world. It follows, then, that the values and related behaviors held by Generation Xers will be substantially different from those held by Baby Boomers.

We can actually take a much longer view and provide a historical reference for this position. Generational identity is not the largest unit to be observed in explaining qualitative differences occurring in Western history. The Greco-Roman Age gave way to the darkness of the Middle Ages, which, in turn, laid the foundation for emergence into the Renaissance. The Renaissance gave way to the Industrial Revolution, which was the forerunner of what is not only the beginning of the Third Millennium: It might also be viewed as the official dawning of the Information Age. If this more radical perspective of the changes we are seeing today prevails, then the differences that exist between Baby Boomers and Gen Xers will become relevant factors in defining the new age.

Much of what has been written and discussed to date about generation differences has been more anecdotal than scientific in nature. An extensive review of the literature supports this conclusion. There are many thoughtful opinion pieces, surveys, and observations, but prior to our research, there was little or no empirical evidence that meaningful differences existed. However, anecdotal evidence can be powerful, particularly when we realize that people base their behaviors on their experiences of the past.

We tested our assumption of the power of anecdotal evidence with a group of participants at a conference of organization development practitioners in 1998. Prior to presenting the results of our research, we asked participants to respond to a series of questions about their perceptions of Baby Boomers and Gen Xers. After being told loudly and clearly by Gen Xers that they did not appreciate the "Gen X" label because it denied the individuality within their age group, we went on to uncover additional, strongly held perceptions that each group had about the other. What was even more intriguing was the strength of those perceptions on subsequent behaviors. While there was only a little consistency in behaviors across the audience, there was an observable link between what was perceived and the actions that followed. For example, one of the individuals who resisted being placed in the Generation X category continued, throughout the session, to point out the generalities of Generation X that did not, in her opinion, apply to her. In so doing, she effectively isolated herself from identity with either group. The behavior did have the desired effect of supporting her individualism; however, it also had the undesired effect of imposing a level of isolation.

By imagining similar behavior in the workplace, with each individual worker making assumptions and then acting on them, we could easily see what might lie ahead for a workplace peopled with the Baby Boomer and Generation Xer mix. Our greatest concern was that Boomers, increasingly in control of organizations as they assume positions of power, would be making decisions on the basis of certain perceptions and anecdotal experiences and that those decisions would have unexpected and undesirable consequences. Xers, for example, might react to Boomer decisions from a very different set of perceptions and anecdotal experiences. Everyone involved would be doing what was right from his or her own point of view, and the organization would never know the cause of its dysfunction. This, certainly, is not anyone's desired way to run a business, but there have not been many options to do otherwise to date. When our research began, there simply were no data on which to make valid assessments of Baby Boomers and Generation Xers in the workplace. In the absence of facts, perceptions prevail. Perceptions become reality for the person who holds them.

The preponderance of literature prior to our research strongly suggested that Baby Boomers are much more team-oriented and concerned with group processes than are the members of Generation X. This suggestion became the focal point for our study because it addressed an area that could be measured, compared, and contrasted. The research question was "Is there, in fact, a qualitative difference in values and outlook between Baby Boomers and Generation Xers with regard to teams?" If, in fact, there was no significant difference in values and objectives separating Baby Boomers from Generation Xers with regard to team development in the workplace, then Boomers could continue to invest significant amounts of organizational resources into building teams, based on their values, because Boomers and Xers alike shared those values.

Alternatively, if a significant difference did exist, then organizational resources are being spent on teams for people who do not care about Boomer-built teams or, worse, are likely to be downright hostile or antagonistic to them. Should this prove to be the case, an organizational Armageddon could be just around the corner.

Given the current emphasis on teams in the workplace, we felt it was critically important that current and future decisions about teams be based on data that describe how things actually are, rather than on an idealistic view about how things should be. A particular set of values and processes proven effective for teams manned by one generation would not automatically justify the assumption that these same values and processes would be as effective with teams manned, at least in part, by the next generation. To us, the question of team-related values held by each generation was both intriguing and significant in terms of future organizational and employee success.

Our study was designed and conducted with the goal of taking a first look at what might be uniting—and separating—Baby Boomers and Generation Xers, the mix that makes up the majority of today's workforce, as well as the workforce for decades to come. The study yielded some important and totally unexpected results. These results constitute the first hard data on differences and similarities between these two generations.

Chapter 1 introduces the differences and describes the research. Chapter 2 introduces the differences between traditional and authentic teams. Chapter 3 presents the four phases of building authentic teams. Chapter 4 looks at the role of the coach in building authentic teams. Chapter 5 shows how to address conflicts in teams by introducing Theory of Constraints techniques, including the application of a "prerequisite tree." Chapter 6 describes adversary relationships on the job and how to halt them. Finally, chapter 7 looks at how our recommendations affect the retention of Generation X employees and the greater stability of workforces and organizations in what promises to be an increasingly dynamic workplace as the twenty-first century unfolds.

CHAPTER 1

Baby Boomers and Generation Xers at Work

*T*he old-timers won't change and the kids won't work!" These words, "fighting words" for some, are echoing through the halls of corporate America and represent a potentially serious threat to workplace effectiveness. This threat comes at a time when American business can scarcely afford to miss a beat, let alone risk a downward slide. In an age of global competitiveness, rapid and continuous change, and technology that is sometimes outdated before it hits the market, we need to capitalize on every available attribute if we want to retain our positions as global business leaders. Our greatest attribute, and potentially our greatest Achilles' heel, is the American worker.

Two age groups currently dominate the world of work: Baby Boomers, born between 1945 and 1962, and Gen Xers, born between 1963 and 1982. These two groups encompass all workers between ages 18 and 55. Evidence is mounting that this mix is not a happy one. Negative perceptions and attitudes abound. Listen to the watercooler or breakroom discussions in any organization in the country and you will hear stereotyping about your own peer group that probably doesn't apply to you and about others that probably doesn't apply to them:

"Did you see how long it took old George to figure out how to program that computer? Man, I could have had that done in ten minutes!"

"So, the kid's here today, huh? Guess he used up his vacation. Next thing you know, he'll be on medical leave!"

Unfortunately, critical business decisions are being made every day on the basis of these perceptions—decisions about whom to train and how to train them, whom to hire or not hire, how to distribute work, and how to retain employees whose skills are critical but who no longer exhibit the loyalty to the organization that once was the norm. If "truth" is in the eye of the beholder, and if our perceptions drive our behavior, then our behavior, as employers and employees, could be driving our organizations toward some serious trouble!

The Power of a Growing Generation

More than 75 million Americans were born between 1945 and 1962. Today, Boomers represent 28 percent of the American population. According to Best's Review (Jaffe, Hunter, Katz, and Taylor 1996), between now and 2015, one American will turn 50 years old every eight seconds. By 2010, there will be an estimated 96 million people over the age of 50. The Boomers' generation is twice as large as that of their parents and twice as large as that of the next generation, Generation X.

Boomers are in positions of power in their organizations, and they are setting policies that will govern the workplace for the next several decades. Their decisions will affect not only other Boomers in the work-place but also future generations of workers who will be expected to abide by their guidelines. What are those guidelines likely to be, and how well will they accommodate the needs of Gen X employees?

Boomers carry with them the legacy of the 1960s: communes and love beads, peace and serenity, love all around. What is less publicized, but perhaps even more prevalent, is the view that Boomers either mirror the values of their parents or attempt to mirror the values of their children. Dr. Morris Massey, author of the popular 1970s video "What You Are in Where You Were When" (see Massey 1986), once labeled Boomers the "Schizo-Generation" to describe their continuous fluctuations between behaviors that reflect the generations before and after their own. More recently, Massey has described Boomers as people who spend a great deal of time explaining each generation to the other, serving as a kind of bridge between their parents and their children.

This is a curious description for a generation that seemed to break all the rules as it passed from adolescence into adulthood in the 1960s and 1970s. However, a closer look at Boomers today will reveal that their underlying value of seeing the world from all sides has fostered a kind of ambiguity in terms of what they stand for. Massey's characterization of the Boomer "schizo" was all too evident in the parent who spanked his or her child for breaking the rules but then immediately rewarded that same child for his or her spirit. Perhaps Boomers who wonder why their Gen X co-workers and children appear not to share any Boomer values need to reflect on the behaviors that these young people see firsthand.

Xers do not wish to perpetuate or embrace this generalized Boomer ambiguity about the world. They seem to relish expressing themselves and what they stand for in clearly unambiguous ways. If they appear to Boomers to be taking strong stands on minor issues, to the Xers it is appropriate that they are, at least, taking a stand.

A New Version of the Protestant Work Ethic

As Boomers increasingly reach levels of legitimate authority within their organizations, the values of their parents have become more dominant. Boomers grumble about the work ethic of younger employees, much as their parents grumbled about long hair and short skirts. The Protestant ethic served as an anchor for the parents of Boomers and began to surface among Boomers in stories of what it was like when they first entered the workforce. Boomers have long been proponents of intrinsic rewards, and job satisfaction as a management concept came of age in the early Boomer era. Now, as Boomers become managers of younger employees, intrinsic rewards more frequently sound like Protestant ethic arguments about how one should behave at work. Boomers often view self-sacrifice in the interests of a job well done to be a norm worth fostering among their peers and subordinates. Comments about workers "not caring" about what they do or "doing only what they have to" clearly revert to the "work as its own reward" concept. It is a message that Gen Xers neither understand nor wish to emulate.

In fact, an opposite stereotype has been applied to Xers. Members of Generation X are viewed as self-centered, not self-sacrificing. Time at work is seen as a means to an end, the paycheck. Work is not their sole purpose in life. The Boomer motto of "living to work" is reversed in the Gen Xer's preference of "working to live." This simple but powerful dichotomy between Boomers and Gen Xers is sufficient in itself to foster significant levels of unproductive conflict.

Contrasting Commitments

Boomer employees and Gen X employees appear to take different paths regarding commitment. Commitment-related workplace behaviors, including overall loyalty to the company, have become sources of conflict and stress between the generations. Boomers, for the most part, adopted the cradle-to-grave mentality modeled by their parents. It wasn't necessarily a conscious choice; it was simply the most obvious choice at the time Boomers entered the workplace. Boomer parents warned against the perils of job-hopping and preached the wisdom of loyalty to one's employer: If you took care of your employers, they would take care of you. As Boomers moved into adulthood and acquired mortgages and children, they accepted the loyalty norm with little or no resistance. Later, Gen Xers witnessed the way their parents' loyalty was rewarded. They saw the devastation of downsizing, right-sizing, process reengineering, and job elimination. They watched, and they learned.

A recent study on worker retention conducted by Walker Information and the Hudson Institute found that only 25 percent of employees today consider themselves truly committed to their organizations and plan to stay two or more additional years. About one-third of the respondents are considered high risk and state that they are not planning to stay for even two years. Another 39 percent say they plan to stay with their current employers, but they describe themselves as "trapped." They feel that they have no option other than to stay where they are.

This lack of commitment is difficult for Boomer managers to accept. Faced with unprecedented high turnover rates, managers find themselves continuously recruiting and training new employees just to ensure continuity of service to customers. Continuous recruiting and training consume time and money. Productivity falters when a significant percentage of a workforce is still on the learning curve. It takes new hires longer to get the job done, and increased errors are more likely. Errors result in rework, or the risk of poor product going to the customer. It has long been a rule of thumb that an employee must be on the job for at least a year before he or she returns any profit to the company. If this is true, we have a scenario in which investment is high and payback is very low.

In addition, new employees are usually trained by existing employees. Training thus reduces the productivity of those experienced employees as well. Added to this is the pressure in almost all organizations today to do more with less. Workers and managers alike live increasingly on the edge of chaos and burnout. Given issues of loyalty and commitment alone, organization survival is at risk. According to the Bureau of Labor Statistics, employee tenure in 1998 was 3.6 years; the median tenure for workers ages 45 to 54 was more than double that of workers ages 25 to 34. Strategic planning thus becomes complicated by a work population that is in a continuous state of flux. Similarly, a workforce that is not uniformly committed to the organization's success increases that organization's struggle to remain viable in a turbulent marketplace. Commitment plays a big part in productivity, in an employee's openness to learn and to do new things, and in an employee's willingness and ability to be fast and flexible on the job. We already know that flexibility and speed are essential for any business enterprise to survive in the twenty-first century. Flexibility and speed no longer guarantee success; they are merely a ticket to play.

Machines and technology contribute enormously to an organization's speed and flexibility, but ultimately it is people who make or break the organization. Without a willing workforce pulling together to fulfill the organization's mission, dysfunction is a logical outcome. Corporation dysfunction has the potential to get worse if Boomers and Gen Xers continue to move in separate directions regarding commitment.

Labor Projections among the Two Generations

As the Baby Boom generation continues to age, the labor force aged 45 to 64 will grow faster than any other group before or after it. Concurrently, the U.S. Bureau of Labor Statistics projects that the labor force aged 25 to 34 will decline by some 2.7 million members. Recent legislation that removes Social Security penalties for workers who continue to be in the workforce after retirement age increases the span of time during which these two generations will be interacting in the workplace.

Between 1998 and 2008, employment is projected to increase by 14 percent, and the supply of workers is projected to increase by 12 percent. As noted above, Boomers will greatly outnumber Xers in the labor force. Two additional trends aggravate the situation. First, aging Boomers want and expect to work longer but do not necessarily want to work as hard as they worked when they were younger. Their vision of the "golden years" includes more flexibility at work, greater intrinsic rewards, and less managerial/leadership responsibility.

Second, the fastest job growth is expected to occur in the computer and high-tech arena, where Gen Xers tend to be more comfortable and more proficient than their older workforce counterparts. The tension between Boomers' worker availability and Xers' worker expertise can potentially further affect workplace effectiveness. A real-life example occurred recently.

*S*am, a senior in high school, went to work part time for a small engineering firm in the area where he lived. Sam was a computer whiz. He could make computers do things that the older members of the firm that hired him could barely imagine. This firm's Boomer managers wanted systems that could do great things for their company, but they didn't want to pay for professionals who at the time charged small companies a considerable amount for their expertise. So the Boomer managers hired Sam.

What was a relatively low salary from the company's standpoint (and from the perspective of an IT professional) was quite impressive to Sam. Not only was he going to get to do what he loved to do (play with computers), but he was going to be paid for it as well. The parties on both sides of the employment equation were happy; the employer's coffers were relatively unscathed, and the employee's pockets were, relatively, lined with gold.

Sam worked very hard. There was no evidence of the "Gen X slacker" stereotype already being applied to others of his age group. Sam was doing what he loved to do, he was creating things to meet the needs of his new employer, and he could tell his employer was pleased. Sam worked in the office as his schedule allowed, and he often brought work home to his basement hideaway, where he worked long into the night to solve a particularly difficult problem or design a challenging application. The employer gave Sam a great deal of freedom to do things his own way.

One of the things that pleased Sam most was that he could go to work in his school-day attire, which included oversized, low-slung jeans with boxers peeking out at the waist. Unlike his parents, who constantly badgered him to pull up his pants, Sam's "cool" boss seemed to think Sam was just fine the way he was.

One day Sam's boss invited him to join the rest of the workers in the office for a "special presentation." Sam envisioned some well-deserved recognition and reward for his hard work. Unlike many Xers, the paycheck was not a reward in Sam's eyes; it was a fair exchange for his labor. What he envisioned was something more personal and meaningful as an acknowledgment of the good job he had been doing. What he got instead, in front of everyone else in the organization, was a pair of suspenders. Sam didn't understand.

Sam's Boomer co-workers did appreciate his work, but they had obviously agreed that his nonconformance to their perception of proper workplace attire was a problem. True, casual dress was the norm at this organization, but their definition of casual was not quite the same as Sam's. Sam was getting paid for his work, but to him a paycheck fell into a different category than appreciation. He expected something personal from his co-workers—an afternoon off with pay, a new computer, maybe even a game he could play when he needed a break from his work. What Sam got instead was suspenders. Shortly after that event, Sam left the job.

Sam wasn't angry with his boss or co-workers, and they were not angry with him. But something had changed. The differences between them had become too visible and too wide. Sam had no loyalty to the company; he felt no obligation to stay other than to have an opportunity to do work that he liked. His tenure was only four months, barely a blip on the screen of this organization's life. While he was totally committed to working on the computer, Sam's commitment to his employer was minimal. To further feed the stereotype of Gen Xers and their "McJob" orientation (moving from one job to another, with the only significant difference between jobs being a geographic location), Sam found another similar opportunity, quite by accident, within two months. That job, too, lasted four months, and Sam moved on once again.

It is easy to imagine Sam's Boomer employers concluding that Sam just didn't want to work. It is equally easy to imagine Sam deciding that the boss really didn't care about him or his work all that much. Of course, such words were never directly spoken; no opportunity for clarification or understanding was sought or provided. Yet, each party acted on its perception, and neither perception was true. Sam wanted to work and was happy doing the work. Sam's employer at the engineering firm liked him and was happy with what Sam produced. But both had expectations based on their own frame of reference. When those expectations were not met, the relationship changed. Sam lost a good job, and his employer lost a good worker. No one came out a winner.

The Evolution of the Baby Boomer

For Baby Boomers, born between 1945 and 1962, the years when they were growing to adulthood were most significant in shaping their behavior. It was during this time, conservatively from age 10 or 12 to 18 or 20, that values were being tested, personal preferences were being explored, and experience and education were helping to shape individual perspectives about the world. Formative years for Boomers range from 1955 to 1975.

The first Baby Boomers turned 18 in 1963. That statement alone tells you a lot about their generation. These first Boomers entered the workforce in the midst of extreme social upheaval. By 1963, the world had been turned upside down.

From the mid-1960s to the early 1970s, Vietnam was a real presence in the lives of Baby Boomers and their offspring. Young men went to war, or they went to Canada. Young women married their sweethearts before shipping them off to fight, often bearing first sons or daughters while husbands were halfway around the world, or they waited for lovers to return. Some never did. For many of those who did return, it was in body only; their spirit was gone. A generation of men and women experienced a life-changing event, either firsthand or through the experience of a loved one, that continues to influence them even today.

Many draw comparisons between Vietnam veterans and veterans of World War II, who returned to civilian life to take on, without apparent emotional trauma, responsibilities once carried by their fathers. That generation carried its wartime legacy with quiet dignity and grace. But the war in Vietnam was wholly unlike the war in Europe and the Pacific. The legacy for veterans of World War II was far more positive, far less destructive, than the legacy of Vietnam. Regardless of political or social arguments about the Vietnam conflict, the reality is that the Baby Boom generation lost the innocence and idealism handed down by their parents.

Lost, too, was respect for authority. The Baby Boomers who went to Vietnam, as well as the loved ones they left behind, came to question the wisdom and direction of the decision makers who had so significantly affected their lives. For many older Boomers, Vietnam struck a blow to that trust and respect formerly given almost automatically on the basis of age or rank. The catch-all phrase associated with the 1960s, "Never trust anyone over 30," was more than the tag line for a group of radicals; it represented a fundamental shift in relationship between those who were in authority and those who were not.

Younger Boomers, those who didn't experience Vietnam firsthand, were left with a different message. In 1973, when the oldest Boomers were 28 and the youngest were just 11 years old, the military draft ended and the United States converted to an all-volunteer army. No one born after 1955 was required to serve in the military, although a selective-service registration requirement was reinstated in 1980 as a hedge against potential future crises. By the time a mandatory draft was again given serious consideration, when Operation Desert Storm unfolded in early 1991, the youngest Baby Boomers were 29 years old.

In the post–World War II era, a military structure dominated virtually every aspect of American business. Most decision makers, almost always men, had experienced some time in a military setting; it was a point of passage to young adulthood. In the military, men learned how to lead, how to maintain control, how to develop a plan, and how to implement it. They learned to respect their superiors and to honor duty to one's country.

Few of these lessons were learned in Vietnam. For young adults in the post-Vietnam era, the military was only one of many options and not the most favored. The emphasis within the spectrum of workplace effectiveness had moved from one that was very structured, with clear lines of authority and responsibility, to one that was largely self-defined.

Today, our observation may be that "kids won't work," but it's quite possible that "the kids" are actually working very hard. They just aren't working in the way their parents and managers expect. Consider the following scenario, one that occurs on a regular basis in offices and factories around the country.

*T*ony shows up for his job a few minutes late but, once on the job, gets right to work on a stack of work orders left for him the night before. He works diligently to finish the stack, then hands them off to the next person down the line. Noticing that there is nothing waiting for him to do, Tony takes a break. He has a soda and spends some time in the breakroom visiting with friends. All in all, he is away from his work station for about an hour.

Tony's Boomer supervisor is furious. She promptly tells Tony that he is there to work for eight hours, not to gab with everyone in the building, and that he will have to make up the time he has lost. Tony's bewildered response is that his work was done before he went on break, to which his supervisor replies that, if he was out of work, he should have looked for more. Tony, even more baffled now, asks his supervisor why she didn't tell him that she had other things she wanted him to do because, if she had, he most certainly would have done them.

From her perspective, Tony's supervisor had a legitimate expectation that he would look for work when his current assignment was complete. That is her work ethic, one she has never questioned. Tony, however, did not even think to look for work elsewhere. His assumption was that his work was done until someone gave him his next assignment. So we have a supervisor, just trying to ensure work gets done, convinced that this kid won't work, and Tony, just trying to do a good job, convinced that no one in management makes sense.

Interactions such as these between Boomer managers and Gen X employees all too often result in misunderstanding. They become fuel for perceptions that serve to drive workplace behaviors even farther apart. These behaviors ultimately consume energy, destroy efficiency, and make effectiveness just a word in the mission statement

New Realities

Most Gen Xers know nothing of the experiences and lessons of their parents' generation, nor are they interested in learning. For a variety of reasons Gen Xers have grown up to be independent and self-sufficient, and hearing about the way things "used to be" just isn't important to them. As a result, the Xer truly cannot fathom the Boomer's perspective. While Xers may have overheard parents and their parents' friends talking about social injustice and equal rights with great passion, by the time Xers were ready to go to work the world looked significantly different. The passion that so many Baby Boomers put into social reform in the 1960s was finally bearing fruit in the mid- to late 1980s and early 1990s. As is so often the case, the recipients of social reform come to take for granted the benefits won by early reformers.

For example, most young women entering the workforce in the mid-1990s and beyond come to the workplace believing they are entitled to any job for which they are qualified. Their male counterparts accept a fair share of household duties; they know how to cook and do laundry, often as a result of their own mothers working outside the home. Children are seen as an equal responsibility of both parents, and sharing in their upbringing is not even a point of discussion.

Consider, however, the effect this new perspective on family life is having on the Boomer managers for whom these young people now find themselves working. If the baby gets sick, Mom or Dad will stay home from work to take care of her. There is often no extended family to which young parents can turn; Grandma lives in another town or has a full-time job of her own, and Grandpa won't change diapers.

When Boomer babies got sick, Mom was usually the one to stay home. If Mom worked, she rarely earned as much as Dad, so it was easy to determine whose job should take priority. In some business circles, it was taken for granted that a woman would never contribute as much as a man in the same position might contribute because she would always have the primary responsibility for family-related problems.

For Boomers, having two incomes was more often than not a choice. If Mom did not want to work, there was little societal pressure for her to do so. Men were the primary breadwinners and ultimately responsible for the

17

financial well-being of the family. We know this scenario did not apply in every family, but for the majority income earned by Mom was a luxury.

For Xers, two incomes is not a luxury; it is a necessity. It is difficult to live today on one income, and health and medical benefits have, in some cases, become more valuable than the salary. The high cost of child care often takes whatever is left of one income after taxes and benefit costs have been removed. If you talk to any group of young working mothers, you will likely find many if not all of them working for benefits and using their paychecks to pay for child care while they work.

Today, when a Gen X mother calls in to say that she will miss work because her child is sick, her Baby Boomer manager is sympathetic. He or she believes, after all, that a mother's place is with her sick child, just as it was when his or her own children were small. However, the manager still must deal with the work that needs to be done. If several young mothers happen to call in on the same day, you are very likely to find their Boomer manager talking about loyalty to the job — and how hard it is to find these days. This never used to be the case. When a woman worked, she made sure she had someone to take care of the kids while she was gone. That, to the Boomer manager, seems a very reasonable and appropriate approach.

Pity the young man who takes his turn at home with the sick kids. The first thought on the part of his manager will often be "Where's his wife?"

It is still hard for Baby Boomers to acknowledge that it may be just as much Dad's job to stay home with a sick child as it is Mom's. The Xer Dad who calls in to say he will be at home with Junior is simply taking his turn with the kids. To his Boomer boss, however, this guy just became a slacker and was thrown into the deep end of the Gen X stereotype pool.

A Different Kind of Loyalty

Gen Xers have strong feelings of loyalty to family and friends. Often described as "latchkey" kids, the first generation of children to come home after school to an empty house because both Mom and Dad were at work, Xers have vowed to make it different for their own children.

This focus can be observed at a high-tech manufacturing facility in the Midwest, where the workforce includes a significant number of Gen

X employees as well as a fairly substantial group of long-term Boomer employees. It is common to see young mothers in the cafeteria with their children, visiting during breaks and lunch periods. An easy assumption by a Boomer observer would be that the mother is not an employee, but just visiting those with whom she used to work. The assumption is often wrong. Young mothers and fathers who work in this facility often take the day off to take care of doctor visits and similar parental responsibilities. These are not responsibilities that Gen X parents are willing to entrust to someone else. In fact, to them parenting is a much higher priority than working in the factory. Anyone can work in the factory. No one else can be a parent to one's own child.

This very admirable value creates challenges that Boomer managers are ill equipped to face. When their children were small, child-rearing responsibilities rarely fell to the father because the mother was either at home full time or in a job where flexibility was high and pay was low. Listening to Boomer supervisors in this facility, mostly male, describe their difficulty in running departments with employees whose values and behavior are so different from their own illustrates the dilemma many corporations today face.

While no one wants to fault a parent for wanting to be with his or her child, a certain level of production is necessary to meet customer demand. When employees are missing, that level can be difficult to meet. And, while the employee who stayed home with a sick child might be back on the job tomorrow, it is highly likely that another Gen X member of the workforce will be missing for what, to him or her, is a perfectly legitimate reason. Where the Baby Boomer sees a slacker, the Gen Xer sees legitimate choices in how he or she spends time. Recent legislation such as the Family Medical Leave Act reinforces the validity of this choice. An obvious solution to this inability to count on steady attendance by members of the workforce is to overstaff. However, the cost of overstaffing in today's world of shrinking margins can put a company at risk in a very competitive, price-conscious marketplace.

Two Mind-sets at Work

Baby Boomers in decision-making roles across corporate America sacrificed personal desire to be with a child or other family member in order to honor loyalty and commitment to the job. For the Gen X employee, this just does not compute.

Baby Boomers who entered the workforce in the 1960s through the 1980s did so with the same cradle-to-grave loyalty to the job as their parents. Large companies had programs designed to develop young professionals through the ranks to high-level positions. These programs were highly coveted. They carried a promise of success by existing standards—a management job and the salary and perks that went with it. Unions that promised high wages and job security in exchange for an honest day's work represented factories and other blue-collar work sites. In some cases, Boomers talked about changing the system from its existing autocratic structure. This rhetoric, however, did not prevent most Baby Boomers from taking roles within the system, abiding by its rules, and reaping its rewards.

Expectations for both employers and employees were met, for the most part, until the late 1980s and early 1990s. Then, global competition and rapidly advancing technology began to change the world of work. Middle management became a thing of the past as corporations took steps to flatten their structures and reduce overhead. Career ladders became crowded, with women and minorities filling positions formerly reserved solely for white males. Where once a white male was considered first for an open management position, this same white male may now find himself considered last. A new term came into being to describe the fate of these individuals. They found themselves at a "career plateau." Sometimes the plateau was permanent. Boomers had played by the rules, and the rules had changed. Generation Xers were waiting in the wings, and they were watching. They vowed to never let it happen to them.

In the midst of this change, Boomers, who sacrificed so much, feel annoyed by a new generation that seems to sacrifice so little yet wants the same things, or more, in return. Boomers worry about who will keep the business going when they retire. They wonder if there is enough time left to instill in this new generation the kind of loyalty that Boomers hold as a testament to their value in the workplace. A planning session with a group of Boomers who had to make a case to keep their function from being outsourced by their organization made this mind-set all too clear.

*F*ifteen employees had long tenure with an organization, albeit in different divisions. They were of various ages and experience, but all fell within Baby Boom parameters. One of the questions this group was required to answer was "Why can you do this job better than anyone else?" The only answer they could articulate was that they had been around for a long time, that they had been loyal to the company, and that they were good at their jobs. This response was consistently met with a resounding "So what?" from the consultant. The baffled look on the employees' faces made it clear that no one in the group could conceive of a greater value than his or her loyalty to and longevity with the organization.

Ultimately the group was able to articulate that "There is enough wisdom and knowledge in this room to do anything, and to do it better and faster, than anyone else in this industry could possibly do." This was, in fact, the true value the members brought to the organization. But it took some effort for them to recognize the value of their knowledge and skills apart from blind loyalty to the organization, even in the face of losing their jobs.

Xers don't care how long a Boomer has been with the company. They know there is another job waiting just around the corner and that no job should come before family and friends. Xers are very loyal, but not to the company. Their relationship with the company is one of service rendered for dollars paid. So long as work does not diminish their personal lives, Xers are more likely to stay with one company. But when work interferes with what is really important to them, Gen Xers put company loyalty dead last.

Family and friends are important to Boomers, too, but family loyalty is demonstrated in a very different way. Boomers believe that by working hard and providing nice things for their families, they are putting family first. For Xers, putting family first means being there. Period. Work should not interfere with family obligations.

In fact, for Gen Xers in the 1990s and beyond, families and friends come first. For example, relative to Boomers in the 1960s and 1970s, who often changed residency for career advances, Gen Xers think that moving for the sake of job alone is not a worthwhile investment when one considers the cost to family and personal lives.

Gen Xer Priorities

Work itself is not a reward for Gen Xers. It is a necessary evil. If, therefore, work can be fun, it can be tolerated. The very things that make work fun for Gen Xers are problematic for their Boomer counterparts: technology, speed, continuous change. Gen Xers want to multitask, then play a video game to relax. To make matters worse, they want to partner with a friend when they do it!

A few years ago, when the earliest Xers were still in high school and college, research was done by a graduate student at Webster University in Chicago on the motivation of caddies at several prestigious golf clubs on the North Shore. All of the clubs competed for caddies by offering a wide variety of pay scales, club privileges, and progressive benefits for the caddies who stayed with a club for more than one season. When parents of caddies were interviewed, they were very conversant with the potential benefits their offspring could realize by caddying at one of these clubs. Their hope was that their child would find the "right" club and continue to work there until he or she had capitalized on what the club had to offer.

What the caddies used to assess the value of their jobs was somewhat different from the criteria used by their parents. Almost to a person, the young people cared about being with their friends and having time to play the course above any other kind of financial incentive. Caddies would not change clubs for a pay increase; they would, however, change and even take a pay cut if it meant they would be able to work with friends who were caddies at another club.

This does not mean compensation is unimportant to the Gen Xer. Stories are rampant about young workers making significant job changes for as little as fifty cents per hour. This, in fact, has fed the "McJob" characterization of employees job-hopping from one low-level job to another with little provocation. However, Gen Xers often view money as an entitlement. This conception is sometimes accompanied by outlandish expectations of the value of what they contribute. Gen Xers, probably more so than any previous generation, fulfill Herzberg's theory of motivation that says money is not a motivator, but the absence of money is a demotivator. For Gen Xers, however, when priorities are ranked, friends always come out on top.

An illustration regarding the loyalty of Gen Xers to friends has to do with snitching, or "narcing," as it came to be known among the drug crowd. No matter what happened, no Gen X teenager would ever rat on a friend. There is evidence of this same loyalty in the workplace today. As with any generation, some Gen Xers (and some Boomers) work harder than others. Boomers will let you know, and quickly, when a peer isn't pulling his or her weight. A Boomer boss who asks a Gen X employee to keep an eye on a co-worker's work habits, however, may be surprised at the employee's response. "No way!" will often be the quick retort, followed by an admonition that it is the boss's job to determine if someone is doing his or her job. The relationship with a co-worker, particularly if that person is considered to be a friend, comes first. Loyalty to the company, or to the boss, is a distant second.

A point of clarification is in order. Not all Gen Xers are close to their families. Growing pains for some Gen Xers caused as many or more family rifts as in any other generation. However, when a Gen Xer is close to his or her family, it is a closeness that carries with it a loyalty that is possibly stronger than any seen in the recent past.

The Transformation of Authority Relationships

There is possibly no greater sore point between Baby Boomers and their Generation X co-workers than the younger generation's lack of respect for authority. For many Baby Boomers, respect for authority on the basis of age or rank was a casualty of the Vietnam era, as was noted earlier. Yet Boomers are still to some degree a product of their parents' values. They were raised to respect their elders, teachers, ministers, government officials, and managers; respect was given to the positions these individuals held, if not to the individuals themselves.

An increasingly well-educated population of Boomers, however, has found it difficult, if not impossible, to accept direction from those who are obviously less informed and less capable than themselves. This group includes not only the elders of the corporation, who continue to work as if nothing has changed, but newcomers as well. Just as social mores have changed under Boomer influence, workplace norms have undergone a significant transformation. The hierarchy has flattened.

23

Management has become more participatory. Social skills are taking on greater credence as valid components of workplace effectiveness. Industrial democracy has become, under Baby Boomer influence, a reality of today's successful business organizations. Boomers have mellowed with age. They are more likely to work within the system to change it through evolution.

However, the role of the authority figure in the lives of Baby Boomers is increasingly paradoxical as time goes by. Boomers were raised to respect authority, but learned through experience that respect was not always justified. Boomers are now becoming authority figures themselves. They are acquiring power through both the legitimacy of their positions and the value of their expertise.

Now, as Generation Xers enter the workplace, the game is changing. Gen X employees, possibly as a result of hearing their parents discuss managers whose actions they disagreed with or disapproved of, almost universally offer respect only to those who they feel deserve it. Respect is linked to another person's willingness to "walk their talk" and to refrain from treating others in demeaning and disrespectful ways. Position, role, or rank alone simply does not count.

Evidence of this can be seen in the many daily interactions between frontline employees and senior managers in more progressive organizations. It is easy to recall the days when no employee would speak to or interact with a senior manager unless specifically invited to do so. Today, many Boomer employees will still have difficulty interacting comfortably with someone whose position is at a significantly higher level than their own. Not so with their Gen X counterparts. At a recent monthly meeting of manufacturing associates designed to give voice to issues on the floor, a request was made for the plant manager to attend the next session so that participants could share with him, in person, the issues that were troubling them. This was not an attempt to bypass their own supervisors; supervisors on the floor were well aware of the issues being discussed. It was, instead, an honest desire to have a dialogue with the highest-level person in the facility. After the invitation was extended, the plant manager, who was not available for the next monthly meeting, arranged to meet with associates within days of that meeting to hear their issues.

By "walking his talk" and making himself available to interact with people at all levels of the facility, this plant manager maintained the respect he had earned previously by taking similar action. Had the manager declined the invitation, Boomer participants in the group would not have given much thought to his absence. They would have assumed that other, more pressing duties had taken priority. The plant manager's credibility with younger participants, however, would have suffered.

A Case of Successful Integration

The real paradox of respect in the workplace today is that both Baby Boomers and Gen Xers are willing to offer respect to those who treat them with respect, as human beings, regardless of rank. Yet, often, no one seems willing to offer respect first or to accept that his or her own actions might generate a lack of respect in others. A third-shift, self-directed work team in a high-tech manufacturing facility struggled with and effectively managed this dilemma.

While self-directed work teams were the organizational structure of choice in this facility, the third shift in particular had done little to create teams. Part of this lack of attention to restructuring was due to chronic turnover in personnel. Typically employees started on third shift but then bid out to second- or first-shift positions as soon as they became available. Another difficulty was the lack of supporting functions on the off-shifts. Human resources, engineering, training, and other support groups did not work three shifts, so finding support for third-shift activities was difficult.

When a new supervisor recognized that this third-shift group had been and was likely to be stable for a period of several months, she took the initiative to introduce self-directed work teams to the shift. The group entered into a very structured development process, used successfully for first-shift teams, and engaged the support of appropriate training and development personnel. As team members progressed through task-focused requirements, they learned a great deal about the strengths each member brought to the team. They also learned how to turn points of conflict into points of discussion and learning.

Their diversity, which spanned gender, national origin, and age, became a source of energy and creativity, as well as the basis for teasing and fun. It was not uncommon for a senior, female member of the group to refer to a young, Hispanic male on the team as a "kid" and tease him about coming in late to work or missing an important assignment. Likewise, younger members of the group acknowledged the differences exhibited by their older co-workers as perfectly understandable, given their age and tenure. Out of these light exchanges, strong bonds developed among all members of the team.

It took the third-shift team a full year to accomplish all of the developmental criteria to reach Phase 4, which was designated "high performance" in this organization's structure. There was a rhythm to what the team did. Work flowed easily, workers pitched in to help wherever help was needed, and, if one member found another member doing something incorrectly, there was no hesitation in offering feedback and assistance.

The team's efforts were rewarded a short time later in very real terms. During a downsizing at the manufacturing facility, a decision was made to eliminate the third shift in all departments in an effort to cut overhead costs. However, after reviewing productivity, it was found that the third-shift team in this particular department outproduced its second and first-shift counterparts, even though there were fewer people on the third shift than on either of the earlier shifts. As a result, the second-shift operation was shut down and the third-shift team was allowed to continue its outstanding performance.

The evidence of how this team initiative had crossed generations to create a meaningful and effective workplace became even more apparent about a year later, with four very telling examples.

• Due to family commitments, a Baby Boom member of the third-shift team transferred to second shift and a new product area in order to be home at night. As she began to participate in activities of the new team, she realized that they weren't very successful, and they weren't approaching team development in a way that would ever allow them to be successful. She immediately began to provide feedback and guidance to help the team get on the right track.

• Another member of the third-shift team left to have her first baby. When she returned to work, she worked on first shift. Shortly thereafter, she, too, began to consult with her new team on how to rise above the bickering and personal acrimony that characterized the team to achieve levels of mutual respect and high performance.

- Another young woman was brought into the third-shift team after it had achieved Phase 4. Team members worked with her to bring her up to the level of the team's performance, from both technical and interpersonal perspectives. This young woman, who had experienced relationship difficulties in previous positions in the facility, became a productive, happy, and strongly committed member of the team.

- A longtime Boomer member of the third-shift team, actively involved in the team's development to high performance, was considering a move to first shift. A position had become available that she was uniquely qualified for, and the enticement of living life on a normal schedule was strong. After much contemplation, however, she ultimately decided to stay with her team on third shift. The reason, she freely admitted, was her belief that her positive experience as a member of this team would be hard to match elsewhere.

A Brief Overview of Our Research

The above story of this remarkable team, which we will revisit in more detail in chapter 4, provides the key to successful integration of Baby Boomers and Generation Xers at work: creating and using a structure that is based on mutual respect and commitment. Simple? Yes. Easy? No. Respect implies not only that we are willing to acknowledge our differences but that we are willing to accept, not judge, them. In this way differences become strengths. Conversely, continued action and reaction grounded solely in perceptions that have no basis in fact have the potential to do damage.

Two years ago, at a conference of organization development professionals, we found our worst fears to be true. Conference participants acknowledged that they were making decisions every day at work on the basis of anecdotal experiences that were often no more than one-time, random events. There was little consistency among the perceptions held by our audience, and there were no well-grounded suggestions for how to integrate the generations effectively. Frustration was high in members of both generations, as was defensiveness in response to some of the perceptions offered.

The research we presented at this conference forms the premise of this book. We have facts about what the two generations are really like; these facts are the first empirical data of their kind. We also have a model for how to manage the integration of Baby Boomers and Generation X employees for maximum productivity and job satisfaction. This, in turn, leads to greater employee retention. Our model is well grounded in theory and has been proven effective in real life.

We will tell you about work teams that not only are high performing but also celebrate the individual without sacrificing the collective. What we have to say isn't revolutionary, but it is exciting. More important, we provide solutions that anyone can apply. We will give you the blueprint. But first, let us give you the facts.

In looking at the incredible differences in background, values, and perspectives that exist between Baby Boomers and Gen Xers, turmoil seems a reasonable expectation. The major problem, however, is not that conflict exists but that it rests in conjecture rather than in fact. There is no question that discord abounds and is growing at a rapid rate; yet each person has a different guess about why it is occurring, and each responds according to his or her own perceptions.

Teams, self-directed or otherwise, have quickly become the dominant organizational structure due to the growing need for interdependent work to achieve complex organizational objectives. This very real business need mandates that Boomers and Xers increasingly work together if organizational goals are to be accomplished. A confounding factor in effective collaboration between the generations has been the lack of empiric data to test what is actually going on.

The issue of generational warfare came to our attention as the result of a seven-page paper submitted by a student as a class assignment. The paper dealt with this student's assessment of a "coming cataclysm" between the Baby Boom generation and Generation X. The paper caught our interest, and a quick review of existing literature led us to the following conclusions:

- All literature to that point was anecdotal.

- The preponderance of literature suggested a difference in values between Baby Boomers and Gen Xers.

- The two groups could be on a collision course.

- Critical decisions were being made with no valid data on which to base them.

In reviewing these conclusions, particularly the last one, an initial research question emerged: "If Baby Boomers are holding top policy-making positions in most organizations and are committed to creating and fostering teams, are they are creating teams for Xers according to Boomer values and thereby courting Xer disinterest or rebellion rather than the collaborative spirit sought?"

What needed to be determined was whether there were any substantial differences between how Boomers and Xers value teamwork. Most of the literature suggests that Boomers are very community oriented and committed to collaborative work, whereas Xers are seen as loners who are more interested in technology than in people. This widespread assumption is best summarized by Loysk (1997), who said, "Boomers feel invincible in a team, where Busters [Generation Xers] work best alone."

If a significant difference exists in how the respective generations value teamwork, then the Boomers need to know this so they can stop creating self-defeating organizational structures, that is, teams for people who don't like teams. However, if there is no significant difference between how the generations value teamwork, then Boomers can proceed as they have been and be assured that Xers will conform within a few years' time. Either way, it is important to find out what's going on right now.

The First Study

Two things were essential to discovering the answer to the above question. First was a wide random sample of people from both generations. Second was a way of measuring each generation's values around team building. Six organizations from both the public and the private sectors contributed participants to this study. The breakdown of the total sample was 189 Baby Boomers and 209 Generation Xers, for a total of 398 participants.

The instrument chosen to measure the team values of the sample was the *Team and Organizational Behavior Inventory* developed by Goodstein, Cooke, and Goodstein (1987). This reliable instrument is composed of four scales, which measure the respondent's Task Orientation (i.e., concern for what the group is working on) and Maintenance Orientation (i.e., concern for how well the group is working together). Under Task Orientation, there are two measures: one for the extent to which one values task completion, and another that measures the skills one has that are needed to complete the task. Likewise, under Maintenance Orientation, there are measures for how much one values group maintenance (i.e., trust, collaboration, openness) and to determine how skilled one is in group maintenance behaviors. A biographical sheet was also developed and given to each participant in the study, with "Date of Birth" being the most important variable.

While all four scales were given, the only scale that really mattered to the study was Maintenance Values, which measures the extent to which one values teamwork. Based on the anecdotal literature, we were unofficially expecting that Boomers would be significantly more team-oriented than Xers. Again, even if the data showed there was no difference in Maintenance Values between the two generations, this was important information as well.

Data from the 398 participants were compiled and statistically analyzed. The results of the study showed that for three of the measures, there were no significant differences between Baby Boomer responses and those of Generation X. The fourth measure, Maintenance Values, did yield a significant difference in results, but not in the direction that was anticipated. That is, the study clearly showed that Generation Xers are significantly more team-oriented than the Baby Boomers!

The Second Study

The second study was designed to nail down another generally held assumption, this time making a hypothesis in the predicted direction. The research question was "Are Gen Xers more individualistic than Baby Boomers, despite their stronger team orientation?" Our prediction in this case was "Yes, they are."

A sample of 417 was gathered from several locations. The instrument used was the *Individualism-Collectivism Scales* developed by Wagner (1995), which is based on the early work of Hofstede in looking at differences that define national cultures. The instrument is constructed of twenty-five Likert-type items, with "strongly agree" and "strongly disagree" as anchors. The items were factor analyzed to yield five dimensions that distinguish between individualism and collectivism. These factors are

- *Competitiveness*: The degree of beliefs about value of competitive success

- *Solitary Work Preference*: The value attached to working alone

- *Self-Reliance*: Having a self-reliant and autonomous orientation

- *Supremacy of Group Interest*: Beliefs about the usefulness of subordination of personal interests to group interests

- *Supremacy of Group Goals*: Beliefs about the detrimental effects of the pursuit of personal goals over group goal

The correlations among the scales making up the instrument suggested that these scales were each measuring different aspects of the individualism-collectivism continuum.

The data were analyzed and yielded significant differences between Boomers and Xers on two of the five scales. For both Scale 3, Self-Reliance, and Scale 5, Supremacy of Group Goals, Xers scored significantly higher in the direction of individualism. Generation X respondents scored significantly higher on the following three items in the Supremacy of Group Goals category:

(#18) A group is more productive when its members do what they want to do, rather than what the group wants them to do.

(#19) A group is most efficient when its members do what they think is best, rather than doing what the group wants them to do.

(#20) A group is more productive when its members follow their own interests and concerns.

While not reaching statistical significance, trends of the other three scales also showed Xers leaning in the direction of individualism as compared to Baby Boomers.

The combined results of both studies yielded a single statement that could easily change the direction of team building, management, and human resource development for the next two decades. Putting the results of both studies together, the conclusion is

Generation X is significantly more individualistic AND significantly more team-oriented than the Baby Boomer generation.

That is, while Xers value teamwork significantly more than Boomers, they are also more self-reliant and see a positive relationship between supporting personal goals and those of the group. (See Appendix A for a complete presentation of the methodology, analysis, and results of both studies.)

Conclusions

In looking at the results of the research, three conclusions can be drawn.

1. The prevalent and traditional perception of Boomers is that they are group-oriented, see teamwork based on commonality of values and interests, and view personal goals as being necessarily subordinate to those of the group. This perception was left intact by the results of the research.

   What got severely jarred was the commonly held view of the Xers. Xers are more self-reliant and honoring of personal goals, but they are, simultaneously, significantly more team-oriented than the Boomers. This unique combination of characteristics and values that defines Generation X suggests that a new paradigm would be more appropriate in building teams and managing people than the one currently in use.

2. Regardless of the differences between Xers and Boomers, Boomers are still here and will continue to be here for quite some time. There are twice as many Boomers as Xers, and they hold the majority of policy-making roles. Boomers will play an active and vital role in the workforce far longer than any preceding generation. They are healthier and have longer life expectancies than any generation before them. In addition, somebody has to fill key spots that would otherwise be left vacant because of the paucity of Generation X members in the workforce.

3. A more attainable objective is needed: Tolerance! The first step toward creating a more tolerant atmosphere is for each generation to recognize just what it is that the other one has to offer. What Boomers bring to the table is experience, a sense of group values, and a long-term perspective. What Xers bring to the table is a focus on the immediate present, a high-tech proficiency, and a balanced view of the importance of work values and of those values arising from other aspects of one's life.

Once tolerance is established as a starting point, how can we develop new managerial strategies and organizational structures that will support Baby Boomer values and Generation Xer values in the workplace, while at the same time integrating members of both groups into effective teams?

The balance of this book is dedicated to exploring answers to this question. We can restructure our work environments to support the efforts of employees from both generations. Each manager who reads this book can find value in the studies we present and integrate our suggestions into the context and culture of his or her own organization.

CHAPTER 2

A Different View of Teams

*T*he finding that Generation Xers are significantly more individualis-tic and significantly more team-oriented than the Baby Boomers sug-gests that team building has to continue to be a priority for most orga-nizations. Team structures meet the needs of the incoming workforce as much or even more than they have for preceding ones. We must now start developing teams for highly individualistic employees with a dif-ferent set of values. This requires a team-building paradigm that differs from the community-based one currently in vogue.

The current mainstream paradigm is called the "traditional model." Community-based, it holds that effective teams are based on common ground and similar interests. The alternative "authentic individual-based model" holds that the most important element in team building is how each contributing member is uniquely different from all other members. The authentic model makes different assumptions about what is neces-sary to reach group effectiveness. Both models aspire to the same end: to have highly effective task teams whose members work well together. They differ in how this end is best achieved. Let's take a closer look.

A Brief Look at the Traditional Team

The traditional organizational team concept has its theoretic origins in the human relations movement that emerged in the 1930s. Its actual point of origin is usually considered to be the Hawthorne studies conducted by Mayo (1919) and Roethisberger and Dickson (1936). Elton Mayo had taken up the cause of the worker as a counter to Frederick Taylor's advocacy of scientific management in 1911. The actual focus on group dynamics leading to team interaction started with the founding of the National Training Laboratories in the late 1940s. This basic model comes from the field of education. It is based on the perceived need to share common values. The traditional paradigm is "normative" and advocates a "one best way" of building teams. It is characterized by several assumptions.

1. Human behavior is subject to certain "laws" of group dynamics and/ or specific directions.

2. These laws and directions are normative, being better than others, and are distinctly preferred to those that go in the opposite direction; for example, Theory Y is far better than Theory X (McGregor, 1957), and democracy is a superior form of leadership to autocracy as advocated by Likert's (1961) principle of supportive relationships, and so on.

3. Because of these assumptions, it is possible to clearly define categories of behavior and to thus assign individuals to these categories in order to deal with them more easily, for example, using the Myers-Briggs™ typology.

4. Individuals and organizations that do not conform to normative values are not maximizing their full potential and, therefore, are subject to training and consulting that is specifically geared to getting them on board, for example, moving toward the 9'9' position in Blake and Mouton's (1964) grid theory.

5. Preferred behaviors are necessary for a group to adopt and foster before it can function effectively as a team. These behaviors include openness, trust, and cooperation.

A typical traditional team emphasizes common values and objectives. There is a norm for getting along well and for maintaining a high degree of trust and shared feelings. Emphasis is placed on everyone participating in all issues that confront the group. Conflict is honored, and attempts are made to resolve it as quickly and effectively as possible. Group cohesion is an important value, and maintaining supportive interpersonal relationships often becomes as important as accomplishing the team objectives. Group cohesion, when taken to the extreme, puts members at risk of groupthink (Janis 1971), wherein individual group members become guarded with their openness for fear that disagreement will interfere with team cohesiveness. When groupthink happens, group cohesion supersedes all other team objectives. All too often, once a standard for effective team behavior is established and current behavior is successfully measured against it, high performance on task objectives falls to second place. The means of achieving high performance has become an end in and of itself. The basic unit of attention is the team.

For the past forty years or so, graduate programs in business and in organizational behavior, as well as consultants in the field, have been using and evolving this traditional model of team development. It has proved successful because it is built on and is consistent with the Baby Boomer values discussed earlier and is also well represented in the values of the generation that came before it.

The Authentic Team

Authentic teams have their theoretic origins in Gestalt psychology, which is based on the work of Fritz and Laura Perls. Although conceived several decades earlier, Gestalt emerged in the early 1960s as a strong counter to traditional psychoanalysis and other therapies that had been based on the medical model, that is, someone is either mentally ill or mentally healthy. Gestalt has frequently been referred to as "therapy for normals" and is based on a personal growth model that explores how people can increase their ability to get what they want. In his last book, Perls (1973) pointed out that perfect therapy can be achieved by the therapist (or by a parent, manager, or coach) by asking only three questions: (1) "What are you aware of, right now?" (2) "What do you want, right now?" (3) "How are you stopping yourself from getting it, right now?"

Premises that differentiate Gestalt therapy from the medical model therapies include the following:

- Mind and body are an integrated system, not separate, unrelated parts of the person.

- The prime value is on self-support, individual responsibility, and making conscious choices.

- The major skill needed to better one's life and to make better choices is increased awareness of what is occurring right here and right now.

- Finishing unfinished business and saying good-bye to things that are gone forever frequently need to be addressed before one can move on.

- At some level, people choose to be where they are in their lives. They also have the power to make other choices.

- Being successful/content/happy depends mostly on one's ability to make and maintain good contact with oneself, the environment, and those in it.

- Each individual, including oneself, is valued for his or her uniqueness, that is, how each person is different from everyone else. This differentiation is predicated on maintaining clear and identifiable boundaries.

- "Acting out" is a positive, rather than a negative, therapeutic function. Experiencing how you are blocking your own growth is infinitely more insightful than merely understanding it cognitively.

While these few distinctions are an oversimplification of the Gestalt approach, they serve to illustrate its thrust and focus.

By the mid-1970s, several organization development consultants and theorists began to see the potential value of Gestalt as a practical model for organizational growth as well as for individual growth. Herman and

Kornich (1977) established the Gestalt approach to organization development in their book *Authentic Management* by applying the basic assumptions and strategies of Gestalt theory to interpersonal contact in the work setting. According to them, effective management was based on the manager being clear, strong, and aware of what was being experienced and observed in the working environment. The term *authentic team* derives from their initial work.

In 1974, the Gestalt Institute of Cleveland began the Organization & System Development Program, a two-year program to train professional organization development consultants in Gestalt theory and practice. Today, there are hundreds of Gestalt organization development practitioners worldwide. While some operate almost exclusively out of a Gestalt frame of reference, others have added Gestalt theory and practice to their existing approach, creating a more individual and eclectic strategy for their interventions. The underlying assumption is that the dynamics that foster personal growth and increased effectiveness in individuals are just as applicable to groups.

A typical authentic team would appear different from a traditional team in its operation. The authentic team, while just as committed to the need for a common objective for members of the team, supports the right of each individual member to hold separate values and to base commitment to team objectives on individual values. The uniqueness of each person is valued by the team.

In order to facilitate understanding and acceptance of different values, an initial step is to deliberately differentiate each member from another. From a starting point of differentiation, the team then explores ways in which it can work together effectively. Rather than imposing a norm of equal participation, authentic teams encourage participation at levels that are comfortable for individual members. Comfort levels, in turn, will be determined by the team members' interest and ability to make meaningful contributions to the team. On an authentic team, there may never be equal levels of participation among members at any one point in time; however, over time, each member will participate in his or her own way at a level that supports a desire to continue to be part of the team.

Conflict on an authentic team is seen as natural, constructive, and the trademark of a healthy team. Conflict is managed rather than resolved. In a high-performing team where conflict is common, consensus is still the preferred way of making team decisions. When a conflict takes too much of the team's time and appears to have become unproductive, a subgroup of team members discusses and addresses the situation and comes back to the full team with a recommendation. The team then either accepts the recommendation or uses it to build consensus around a new suggestion emerging from the subgroup's work.

The way in which conflict is viewed by an authentic team is that cohesion is a by-product of individual identity and openness and that trust is strengthened by honest differences of opinion, a sort of collective individualism. Collective individualism is not the objective but, rather, the means by which an authentic team achieves high performance.

Herman (1974) and Karp (1998) have identified twenty-one distinctions between the traditional and authentic approaches to organization development. The traditional positions are more consistent with the values that are associated with Baby Boomers. The authentic positions appear much more identified with Generation Xers. This is not a matter of mutual exclusion but, rather, a question of which options the respective generations feel more comfortable with in light of current research.

Nine distinctions have particular relevance to the role of the individual team member in the development of effective work teams.

1. **Traditional:** Interdependence is the key value.
   Authentic: Individual autonomy is the key value.

While interdependence is clearly valued in the human relations traditional approach to team building, it is considered an option from the Gestalt perspective, which views autonomy and individual choice as higher values because ultimately the individual must answer for his or her choices and actions. Gestalt theory, however, also recognizes working interdependently as a valid option.

2. **Traditional:** Experimenting with new process behaviors is preferred.
   Authentic: Increasing awareness of existing behaviors is preferred.

While experimenting with new ways of interacting with team members to better working relationships is beneficial, it is frequently premature. Often this is a case of attempting a solution before the problem is clearly defined. It is far more important for team members to become aware of how they are presently interacting. They can then determine the effects of those interactions and form appropriate responses to them.

3. Traditional: Good work is a result of good working relationships.
Authentic: Good working relationships are the result of doing good work together.

This is not a play on words; it's more a matter of which is the "cart" and which is the "horse." The traditional view concentrates on developing more supportive relationships, such as building trust, cooperation, and openness among team members. The reasonable assumption is that work will progress at a rapid and effective rate due to team members having more supportive working relationships. While this makes sense at first, it also creates problems. Alongside trust is mistrust. Alongside cooperation is self-interest. Alongside openness is the desire for privacy. If a team is operating out of a normative stance of how it "should" be, it is following a set of externally imposed values.

Everyone on the team accepts externally imposed values at different levels. The natural tendency of individuals to mistrust, operate out of a sense of self-interest, and seek privacy will be suppressed. This collusion to repress negative attitudes detracts from group effort.

Alternatively, if the focus is on the work itself, and the group deals with interpersonal issues only when they surface and detract from group effort, more energy goes into performance. High levels of performance increase the team's probability for success. The paradox here is that successful workers tend to appreciate each other as individuals more.

4. Traditional: Appropriate behavior is determined by conformance to team norms.
Authentic: Appropriate behavior is determined by individual choice within each situation.

The key to the authentic approach and, to some extent, Generation X values, is that people rely on their own sense of what is appropriate rather than on someone else's. This does not imply that group norms should not be recognized and adhered to. What it does imply is that group norms need to reflect the values of the individuals making up the group. It also implies that when there is a conflict between what the individual sees as appropriate and what the group sees as appropriate, the individual makes a choice about how to respond consciously, rather than blindly conforming to the group standard of behavior.

5. **Traditional:** Responsibility and rewards are best viewed in terms of team effort.
   Authentic: Responsibility and rewards are best viewed in terms of individual effort.

The thrust in most traditional groups is to create a strong team identity even to the exclusion of maintaining individual identities. This has been encouraged more and more through the use of team rewards. The authentic approach to teams also recognizes the positive aspects of team identity and the need for group cohesion but insists that team identity and cohesion be based on recognizing the uniqueness of each individual that makes up the team. The word *responsibility* literally means the ability to respond and can only be assigned on an individual basis. One can say that the team lost the game, but unless the game is analyzed on the individual level, little opportunity is available to improve overall performance. Outstanding individual effort must be recognized even if team results are less than expected.

6. **Traditional:** Values conflict resolution.
   Authentic: Values conflict management.

The traditional view sees conflict as a necessary but negative force that is unavoidable and seeks ways to constructively eliminate it. If "consensus" is good, then that which destroys it must be bad. The Gestalt view is that conflict is a good way for strong people to work together. It is the prime source of energy and creativity for most groups.

7. **Traditional:** Attempts to empower others.
   Authentic: Recognizes only self-empowerment.

Empowering others is one of the more popular traditional team values. To think that any one individual can have an empowering effect on another individual is really to assume some godlike characteristics.

Gestalt theory asserts that the only person one can ever truly empower or disempower is oneself. Power in its simplest form is really the ability to get what is wanted from the environment, given what is available. You can encourage others, authorize others, assist others, or just get out of their way, but the one thing you can never do is empower others.

8. Traditional: Values being "open."
Authentic: Values being "up-front."

Openness is one of the key identifying values of the traditional approach to team building. Openness says that I will tell you what I am thinking and/or feeling at all times, with the implication that I will hold nothing back. Gestalt puts a much higher value on being up-front than on being open, with the implication that the right to individual privacy takes precedence over the team's right to know: By being up-front I will choose to tell you what I want to disclose, and you can count on what I choose to tell you as being honest.

9. Traditional: The effective team leader/coach puts the welfare of the group before his or her own welfare.
Authentic: The effective team leader/coach looks to his or her own welfare first.

The willingness to place the good of the team ahead of one's own needs is one of the most admired traits of a traditional leader and is highly representative of Baby Boomer values. The authentic view is diametrically opposed to this notion and holds that the pragmatic leader looks to his or her own self-protection first. This does not imply a disregard for the team or that actions will be taken that are in any way self-serving and at the expense of the team.

There are at least three benefits to the team leader/coach checking in with his or her welfare first. One, people are going to be reflexively self-protective anyway, no matter who says that they should or should not be. This position, since it is natural, needs to be legitimized. Two, if there is a threat or danger to the group, the leader/coach will probably sense it as a personal threat first. Unless the leader gives her- or himself permission to respond to a perceived threat at a personal level, she or he is not likely to sense potential danger and be able to warn the team or work with the team to avoid it. Three, if the leader/coach is the sole resource for the team's needs, by being self-protective the leader is also protecting the team's sole resources, and, therefore, also taking best care of the team. This is much like the flight instruction on commercial airplanes that says, "In case of emergency, secure your oxygen mask first; then see to your child's." If the situation calls for increased risk or a measure of self-sacrifice on the part of the leader/coach, this is fine — as long as the choice is made consciously, the potential gain is worth the risk taken, and the choice is seen as being a response to gaining an object rather than a merely virtuous act.

A Different Team-Building Paradigm

At the heart of traditional team building are normative concepts such as Theory Y, consensus decision making, and a collaborative approach to conflict resolution. Team development seeks to realign team members around a strong group identity. Individuals align around their common attributes to form a team whose members essentially share similar values and perspectives. Individual attributes are played down, or repressed, for the good of the team. Group rewards are offered, rather than individual rewards, and the universal motto is "There is no 'I' in team." Figure 1 illustrates the typical entry conditions for a newly formed team.

The team leader, #1, is a little Theory X-ish in his assumptions, member #2 tends toward Theory Y, member #3 is a strong advocate of Theory Z (Ouchi 1981), member #4 is Gestalt-based, and member #5 is a little confused about the whole thing.

The traditional consultant or team facilitator enters and starts working with the group boundary from a normative frame of reference. The group is the basic building block. The goal is that all group members will begin pushing in the same direction from a commonly held theory base and set of values — in this example, Theory Y. A vision of what a team "should be" is held by all and the group works toward that model as a process objective.

The authentic approach to team building takes a different approach. It begins by working with the individual boundary as the basic building block. This means that each member is encouraged to become more

FIGURE 1 *Entry Conditions*

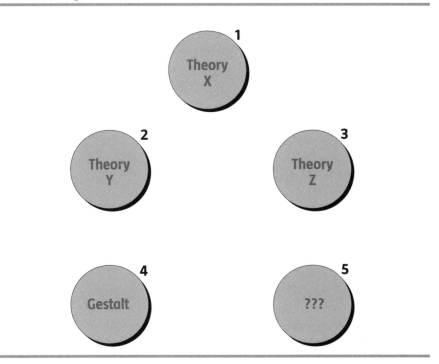

appreciative of how each team member is different from, rather than similar to, the others. Thus, member #1 become more clear about his Theory X beliefs, member #2 more clear about Theory Y, and so forth.

Once individual team members are clearly differentiated, team construction occurs through developing connections among the members from their respective positions. All things considered, a team composed of strong, differentiated individuals has a higher probability for task effectiveness than does one that is composed of people who are trying to be alike. The one similarity that is as critical for authentic teams as for traditional teams is that everyone on the team is equally clear about, and committed to attaining, the team objective(s).

In contrast to the traditional approach (figure 2), the authentic approach creates "snap-away" linkages that allow individuals to work in isolation, in configurations of smaller groups, or as a total team, depending on the task at hand (figure 3). This linked individuality also allows members to enter and leave the team without significant negative effect on

FIGURE 2 *Traditional Team Paradigm*

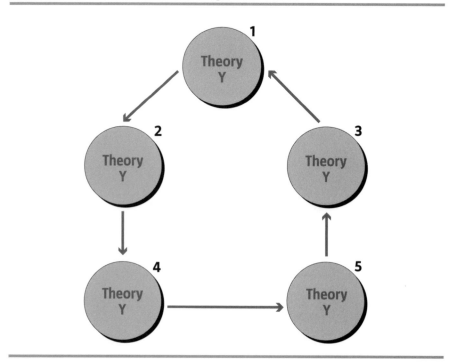

the team as a whole. New members don't have to learn and adopt a "party line" but gain acceptance by simply being more fully who they are.

Implications

Many Gestalt-centered consultants and facilitators advocate the use of the authentic paradigm for all team-building functions, regardless of generational identity, because it deals with people as they are, rather than how they should be, and works from there. The traditional paradigm tends to take an optimistic view of people, and the authentic paradigm tends to take a more pragmatic view. When reviewing research results and contrasting the values and options that separate traditional from authentic, the authentic team-building paradigm appears much more suited to Xers than the traditional.

FIGURE 3 *Authentic Team Paradigm*

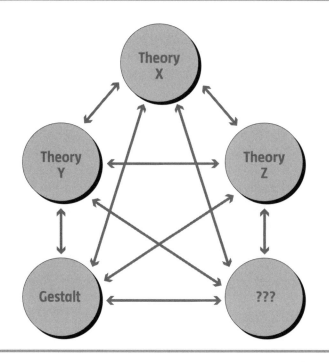

There is nothing wrong with either paradigm, and little can be gained by engaging in argument about which is better. It is reasonable, however, to assume that, on the whole, Boomers would more closely identify with the traditional model and Xers with the authentic. This assumption does present a problem in that most teams are made up of members of both generations.

A necessary solution, at minimum, would be that all team members tolerate the value system of the other generation—and other members. That tolerance must exist before any progress can be made.

Academic Model

A good example of how the basic tenets of authentic management work is found in academic departments in colleges and universities. It isn't reasonable to call any faculty a "team" because most faculties are made up of independent experts who have a strong penchant for autonomy. Therefore, academic freedom is a strongly held value. For team building to be appropriate, there must be a state of interdependence, an objective that can only be accomplished by people working interactively. Teams, as a result, are foreign to the academic environment, where each individual faculty member designs, conducts, and evaluates his or her own classes and research.

In an academic setting, what seems to work best is to encourage each member of the faculty to focus on his or her strengths. That is, those who are excellent researchers may have a reduction in their teaching load to allow them to spend time on their research. And, those who are excellent instructors may not be required to produce the same level of publications that their more research-oriented colleagues are required to do but may carry a heavier teaching responsibility. Those who teach well but have little interest in research or community service will often take on the committee work and similar types of assignments that are necessary to keep the university's infrastructure operating well. This type of organizing, collective individualism, requires that differentiation precede integration. That is, before people can be assigned to a role that maximizes their contribution to the overall objective, their talents, interests, and values must first be identified and honored.

Although there are no teams per se within a university faculty, a type of teamwork does occur in a snap-away structure (as illustrated in figure 3). Two colleagues may collaborate on a publication, each bringing their respective skills to the task, or several colleagues may choose to design and team-teach a course. An entire department may act in concert when going through an accreditation process, with each member contributing and coordinating efforts to achieve the final objective. These are examples of situational alternatives consistent with collective individualism rather than a response to a norm that requires everyone to work together.

A common professional stereotype is that each faculty member is a prima donna with a very delicate ego. Whether ego is the cause or not, conflict is certainly abundant within faculties. Personality differences, political differences, and philosophical differences are just a few of the sparks that ignite the conflict, and the conflict is also what sparks creativity. How conflict is managed within a department can make or break the department, regardless of the talent it contains. Fortunately, it is not a requirement for faculty members to all like each other in order to achieve the objectives of the university.

Sports Model

Professional sports provide another opportunity to look at how the traditional model of a team differs from the authentic model. The most glaring differences are those that exist between the underlying values and practices of the NFL (National Football League) and those of the NBA (National Basketball Association) (Seabrook 1997).

The NFL is a prototype of traditional values. Players are almost anonymous: eleven men dressed alike, wearing masks. The only thing that differentiates them is the number on their back. Each player knows exactly what his role is and is expected to perform it regardless of what he might have to endure in the process. Sacrifice for the good of the team is highly valued, and nearly every score is the result of players collaborating in a precise, orchestrated way. Football mirrors the corporate ethic of the 1950s: centralization, division of labor, doing what you're told (Seabrook 1997, p. 48). The biggest supporters of the NFL are Baby Boomers.

The NBA operates somewhat differently. While basketball is a team sport, the NBA recognizes and celebrates individual contributions. There is a spirit of rebelliousness in the NBA that does not exist in the NFL; there has never been a Dennis Rodman in the NFL! Basketball superstars are supported and set up by other team members, and individual performances are what the game is all about. Self-sacrifice is not a strategic part of the game; doing whatever it takes to win is. The NBA is far more in line with the values of Generation X.

The differences between the NFL and the NBA are reflected in the relationship of values between Boomers and Xers. "Today's sports marketing is about the face, the individual, the personality" (Seabrook 1997, p. 47). The NFL is increasingly concerned about the growing lack of support by Gen Xers, who prefer the NBA, and is actively seeking ways to reverse the trend.

Conclusions

From the authentic position, it is expected that each individual team will be as unique in its characteristics, norms, and values as is each individual member that makes up the team. There can be no "magic template" or set of rules to follow that will guarantee success. Some things to consider, however, when making choices about how to approach the team-building process follow.

First, Xers will be less interested in "warm fuzzies" than Boomers. Don't force them on the Xers or deny them to the Boomers.

Second, the authentic paradigm will be more tolerant of Boomer values than the traditional paradigm will be of Xer values.

Third, Boomers tend to need group identity, whereas Xers are more interested in the emergence of individual relationships. The team can provide both. The authentic model is more flexible than the traditional one and is probably more suited to changing structures like project or matrix organizations.

Fourth, the opportunity to have fun on the job is really important to Xers and may be "catching" for the Boomers. Find a workable level. Make working as an entire team a situational alternative rather than a norm. Some work may best be done in subgroups or by an individual. Research indicates that Xers are more results-oriented than process-oriented. Xers will deal with process issues in terms of how those issues influence achievement of the team's objectives.

Keep in mind that not everybody on the team will like everybody else, no matter what you do. Make it safe for people not to like each other by only intervening in interpersonal relationships if they negatively affect the work.

Finally, remember that loyalty is a value for Boomers and a response to how one is dealt with by Xers. If the requisite amount of loyalty isn't there, find out what's happening to cause that.

CHAPTER 3

Building Authentic Teams

For the next thirty years, there will be both Baby Boomers and Generation Xers in the workplace. This is due, at least in part, to a shrinking labor market. There will be fewer Gen Xers to fill jobs vacated by Baby Boomers. As a result, Boomers will remain in the workforce far longer than was once projected. While the roles that Boomers take at work may change as priorities shift with age, it remains obvious that a new type of organizational structure must emerge that will allow employees from different generations to work together effectively. Ideally it will be a structure that accommodates the needs of all involved without violating the rights of any, a structure that allows people to be both fulfilled and productive.

Work teams in one form or another have been touted as the ideal structure for the rapidly changing, chaotic world of the twenty-first century. We agree. With work teams, organizations can achieve maximum flexibility and commitment to organizational objectives. However, teams can do more than that. Teams can also provide an opportunity to build individual strengths and an outlet for individual creativity. Membership in a high-performing team can bolster self-efficacy and, in turn, lead to increased productivity and profits for the organization. Work teams also provide a bridge to the future. As the generation mix becomes more pronounced, effective personal interactions at work will become more challenging and more important than ever to organizational success.

The kinds of work environments created by authentic teams will help ease the transition from one generation to another and manage the necessary overlap of generations. In fact, if we view work teams not as an end in themselves but as a means to an end, the challenge they represent becomes more worthwhile. This perspective removes work teams from the realm of flavor-of-the-week management technique and places them squarely in the role of transition vehicle. Work teams are the means by which the workplace of the twentieth century will evolve into the workplace of the twenty-first century.

Discussions of moving from hierarchical organization to a flat structure have been in vogue, but the actual transition is less evident. This may be true because Baby Boomers, as they have reached positions of power, have continued many of the traditions of their predecessors. A majority of the workforce still found comfort in the hierarchy. However, as Xers increasingly enter the workforce, lip service to a change in organizational structure will no longer suffice. A large-scale organizational rebirth is needed. Building authentic work teams can accomplish this.

Building an authentic team is not the same as team building. Team-building activities abound, yet effective teams are still hard to find. In the evolution of work teams, a notion has been perpetuated that team-building activities render a group of individuals a team, or that working together on a given project or task creates an instant team, or that belonging to the same department is the same as belonging to a team. In organizations around the country, any and every group of people who work together for any purpose or period of time is called a team. And in organizations around the country, these so-called teams are failing.

One example of team building that is at best temporary is the Outward Bound® experience many work groups engaged in a few years ago. Work groups would sign up for a day or more of strenuous outdoor exercises that required the group to coordinate its activities. The programs were well designed and, during the exercises, most groups did reach a point of being able to work well together. Sessions usually included discussions about how to apply what the group had learned back at the workplace. For a while, the work group's ability to function effectively on the job would improve. There are, however, few examples of this type of team building in and of itself creating and sustaining high performance over a significant period of time. In fact, research has shown that teams that have a defined period of time in which to accomplish their task will typically coalesce and start working together effectively at the chronological midpoint of their efforts, regardless of prior team development activities (Gersick 1991). This short-term, event-driven team success is quite different from the sustained high performance demonstrated by an authentic team.

There are two important and rarely mentioned reasons why teams fail. First, the term *team* means different things to different people. In the face of positive expectations that are unmet and possibly negative expectations that are met, failure is likely. Second, regardless of intent or desire, few people actually know how to systematically create a team that can sustain high levels of performance over a significant period of time. Books abound, as do consultants, yet the failure rate for teams is high. A team is successful only when it lives its values every day. A book can't live team values, and neither can a consultant who is a guest of the organization at best.

Our objective in this book is to show you how to create and sustain authentic teams, teams in which each individual team member is allowed to be who he or she is in real terms and members' talents and abilities are encouraged and enhanced through everyday operation of the team. We are talking about changing the way people interact with one another and, at the same time, about accepting one another in our authenticity. One does not happen to the exclusion of the other. In fact, they happen hand in hand.

We will begin by giving an overview of each of the phases of team development using the forming, storming, norming, performing framework first introduced by Tuckman (1965). Then we will talk about the specific aspects of each phase that foster authentic teams and compare and contrast the likely reactions of both Gen Xers and Baby Boomers to each phase. A detailed description of each phase and what is needed to navigate the phase successfully is provided in Appendix B, "Team Development Timeline." The processes described are both prescriptive and structured, particularly in the early stages of team development. We believe this structure is absolutely necessary for a successful outcome: a long-term, high-performing work team.

For organizational success in the twenty-first century, lessons of the past must be unlearned. In their place, a whole new set of behaviors at work must be adopted. What can happen intuitively when a team is under pressure cannot be sustained over time. The specific behaviors required to function effectively in teams at work must be learned.

Consider again the analogy of a sports team. Every successful sports team spends a great deal of time learning about effective interaction, individual players' strengths and weaknesses, and new plays and methods for "process improvement." Even when a team is at the top of its form, team members do not stop practicing. If a player leaves one team and joins another, he or she must learn different ways to interact, contribute, and communicate. We graciously allow new players or new teams some time before we begin to judge sports performance. Yet we continue to expect work teams to perform without taking time to learn and to practice.

Our model for building authentic teams is similar to that of creating effective sports teams, but there are some significant differences. Sports teams get to choose their members; work teams quite often do not. Coaches of sports teams are selected because of their excellence in coaching; coaches of work teams are often former supervisors with a title change. In sports teams, the range of ages is fairly narrow; at work the opposite is true. Authentic teams are built and sustained in an environment in which co-workers are not always friends and coaches are not always good teachers and facilitators. In many ways, this environment is the reason the structure we propose for building authentic teams is so important: The structure can help bridge the gaps that are organizational realities.

Many of us learn most successfully when some kind of structure is combined with hands-on experience. As a work team becomes more experienced, some of the structure falls away and is gradually replaced by day-to-day operational activities that are somewhat unique to each team, even among teams that work for the same company, in the same area, and on the same general products and functions. This change is entirely appropriate and makes working with teams much more fun. We are not creating cookie-cutter work teams; rather, we are using a structure to provide the strength that a team needs during its development, so that it can be a fully functioning, highly effective adult team. On such a team, members are both willing and able to do the job, and they do it consistently well over time.

Phase 1: Forming

A work team is first of all a group; it is a collection of individuals who have come together for some shared purpose. Whether that purpose is to build a cathedral or to make enough money for next week's groceries, each person has a reason for being there. Yet each person may not know why he or she has been asked to join a group. Individual team members want to know how it benefits them to be a part of the team, not only in the beginning, but also throughout the team development process. It's equally important to be able to link each member's personal goals with the organization's goals. There are legitimate limits to what an individual is willing to give "for the good of the cause." There are fewer limits, however, when what's good for the cause is also good for the individuals working for the cause. That it's okay to identify "what's in it for me" as a member of a team is one of many differences between traditional and authentic teams. As we look at meshing two (or more) generations in the workplace, it becomes even more critical to help individual team members clearly identify personal benefits in being part of a work team.

Phase 1 is the starting point for team development, the "forming" stage in group development. In this phase team members begin to explore new ways of looking at their work and at each other. While there may be some initial resistance, Phase 1 is for the most part quiet and uneventful. Some people are excited about trying something new, especially younger members of the team, who may be more familiar with a team structure and find it comfortable. Others, particularly those who have been around for a while, typically take a wait-and-see attitude. For them, keeping their heads down and maintaining a low profile is the best possible approach. One of the many challenges in Phase 1 is to draw out these diverse opinions and responses so they can be used to help the team move forward.

One theory of group development, known as Cog's Ladder, labels Phase 1 as the polite stage. Observations of a Phase 1 team validate that label. Team members typically raise their hands and wait to be acknowledged before they speak. If they inadvertently interrupt someone else, they quickly apologize. Open disagreement is virtually nonexistent, and opposing points of view stay well hidden. It is easy to be lured into believing that a team is going to be immediately successful when Phase 1 behaviors are observed. However, the politeness will eventually give way to dissension; it has to if the team is to develop the strength required for sustained high performance.

The best idea to stay focused on during Phase 1 is learning. For everyone on a new team, team interactions will differ from previous team experiences. It is important to learn as much as possible about what it means to be on this team, to work on acquiring the necessary skills team members will need to interact effectively, and to get up to speed on new work-related skills. In Phase 1, people need to be approached as if they were being assigned to any new task at work. They don't know what to do, they may not want to do it, and they must be taught how to do it if they are to do it right. In far too many cases this learning curve is barely given consideration. Organizations know that people need time to learn new task skills; they forget that people need time to learn new interactive skills as well.

In the interest of creating teams that are authentic, Phase 1 is also an opportunity to learn more about the individuals on the team. Remember that, at this point, the "team" is only a collection of individuals, each with a distinctive background, experience, education, interaction, knowledge, and set of skills. The first step in building an authentic team is to find out what those differences are—not so that they can be melded into one strong unit, but, rather, so that they can be synergistically linked to form a dynamic force for effectiveness. An effective team is often described as demonstrating "a whole that is greater than the sum of its parts." Keep in mind that the "whole" is not created in Phase 1, but that the seeds planted here will bear fruit later on.

Phase 1 Strategies for Success

In Phase 1 it is usually evident to members that team activities are separate from their "real work." This is a cultural artifact of a workplace that is totally task-focused, the kind of workplace to which most employees have been conditioned. Anything not directly task-related is seen as "outside" the purpose of the job. In Phase 1, team members have probably not given much thought to what's in it for them personally and so may not fully support the team idea. Two things facilitate the integration of team activities into real-work routines.

First, structured team meetings held on a regular schedule are imperative. Do not allow meetings to be cancelled or agendas to be absent. Do keep meetings to a defined period of time (one hour is recommended), and learn to accomplish the team's business in that period. Over time, attending the team meeting does become a part of the team members' work routines. After the newness of a team wears off, meetings are often viewed as an interference to getting real work done; the excuses to cancel a team meeting can be creative in the extreme, especially as the team goes through Phase 2, but team meetings are the anchor for team effectiveness. It is therefore critical to establish commitment to team meetings early on in each team's development and to not waver from this commitment.

Second, begin to link tasks (real work) to team activities by integrating tasks into team development. For example, make it a Phase 1 team task to develop a mission statement and guidelines for how the team will function. Most organizations today, at least the good ones, are task-driven, and their employees are task-focused. Make building the team a concrete task by identifying critical steps for each phase of team development and then completing them. Recognize and reward the team early and often for completion of its team-related tasks, particularly when they can be linked to accomplishment of the team's real work.

Recognition of early successes gives a great boost to the team and builds strength to take on greater challenges in the future. Recognizing success, however, requires (1) setting an objective, (2) working toward that objective, and (3) celebrating when the objective is met. Then the team is aware of why it is being recognized and can use achievement of one goal to provide incentive and guidelines for achievement of the next. Celebrating meaningless goals just for the sake of celebrating only adds to the belief that team activities are outside of what is really important. However, using Phase 1 as an opportunity to set meaningful objectives for the team helps create a solid foundation for what lies ahead.

Manage expectations for Phase 1 realistically. Typically, no big leaps forward occur in this phase, although there may be some successes that cause the team to feel that it has arrived at full effectiveness in record time. While some teams will complete projects with phenomenal success, the success is usually short-lived. Periods of high performance are rarely sustained over time simply because the necessary skills have not yet been fully developed and integrated into the team's way of doing business. A Phase 1 team should enjoy any successes it experiences but should also realize that there is still a long way to go.

There are a number of activities a team can undertake in Phase 1 to help its transition to becoming a fully functional work team. Many of these activities are designed to teach good meeting skills and to clarify the structure of the team's work. Appendix B, "Team Development Timeline," outlines examples of these activities.

Individual styles are explored in Phase 1 both informally and through the use of formal style-analysis instruments such as the DiSC® and MBTI® assessments. Very little of this activity is threatening, but it can be uncomfortable for members of both generations. Many people consider such activities a waste of time, whereas others actively seek out such opportunities to have a better understanding of themselves. When using instruments for self-analysis, it is important to use them only as a tool for understanding, not as an excuse to judge or criticize others.

Although the use of such instruments can be productive, implementing them can consume a considerable amount of time. Remember that in Phase 1, team members have dual accountability for their jobs and their team activities. In Phase 1, teams are extra work; they sit outside of and in addition to what one gets paid to do. It is helpful for a company to staff according to the time demands of team development so that organizational goals and customer commitments are not compromised. This type of manpower planning also sends a clear message about the importance of teams.

Recognizing Transition to Phase 2

As the new team works through its Phase 1 tasks, two things happen. First, individual autonomy is encouraged through attention to personal styles and team member differences. Phase 1 explores what gives each individual member his or her strength as a team member and discovers ways in which differences can complement one another to form team strengths. Second, the routine of team meetings and training becomes less exciting and feels more like interference in day-to-day operational activities. Boomers just want to go back to doing their jobs, and Xers want to move on to something more exciting. The time it takes to reach the end of Phase 1 varies from one team to the next, but it eventually happens to every team that is long term rather than short term in nature.

Symptoms that the team is moving out of Phase 1 and into Phase 2 are clear if you know what to watch for. Look for these developments:

- People stop coming to team meetings. All of a sudden, they have other, more important things to do. Meetings get postponed or cancelled altogether. Decision making becomes difficult because there are few meetings where all team members are present.

- Conflicts begin to pop up. Making differing opinions known suddenly seems to be a popular pastime for team members. Subgrouping, which occurs when groups of two or three unite against other groups of two or three, becomes obvious. Rather than differences being viewed as a source of strength, they become reasons for inclusion or exclusion. When a once-polite group of employees starts to behave like a collection of armed and opposing camps, the team is well on its way to Phase 2.

Phase 2: Storming

In group dynamics, Phase 2 is called "storming." And so it is with teams as well. Phase 2 is the make-or-break stage of team success. The development of individual team members consumes considerable energy in Phase 2. At this point, organizations should expect a dip in productivity and a lack of focus on work; interpersonal conflict will be at its highest level. Members of high-performing teams look back on Phase 2 with mixed emotions. To a person, they would not wish to relive the phase. Yet it is in Phase 2 that the group becomes a team. If a group of individuals is viewed as undergoing a metamorphosis that renders it a fully functioning team in the end, it is during Phase 2 that it develops the strength to emerge successfully.

As the group does its rendition of a butterfly beating its wings against the cocoon to emerge in a more exquisite state, support for its journey will make the difference between team success and team failure. Success or failure of the team is inextricably linked to success or failure of individual team members. Phase 2 consumes a tremendous amount of organizational and individual resources and often returns little of tangible value. This reality must be factored into the role of the team within the larger organization. Phase 2 is not a highly productive phase. As we will see in Phases 3 and 4, however, the payoff for successful passage through Phase 2 is high.

Several components of authentic teams can help ease the storming of Phase 2. Team members need to be encouraged to be aware of and responsible for the behavior they use with one another, as well as the consequences of that behavior. It is common in Phase 2 for team members to seek out the formal leader or coach to make decisions, rather than seek to resolve issues themselves. Moreover, those who were on the fence about the value of teams come down solidly on the side that says teams are a waste of time. Those who were supporters of the concept before hold fast to the concept, but they project considerable animosity toward teammates who, in their opinion, are making the concept impossible to implement. Fairly early in Phase 2, most members of the team would be quite happy to see the team go away.

Authentic teams propose that appropriate behavior is determined by individual choice in each situation encountered by the Phase 2 team. It is absolutely critical for the team to have a strong central figure during Phase 2, whether that person is a team leader, a facilitator, or a coach. That individual's most important role is to deflect back to the team members, and to the team as a whole, ownership of their own behavior. A team of women experiencing the dysfunction of Phase 2 clearly demonstrates the difficulty of this struggle (see next page).

The individual who is the central figure during Phase 2, the coach or team leader, can expect to feel fairly abused. His or her only defense is to avoid being sucked into the fray whenever possible. This does not

*P*rior to the introduction of the new team, a very strong supervisor who was decisive about daily operations had led this group. The team members, all women, had a history of difficult interpersonal relationships that the supervisor had resolved swiftly and decisively. In Phase 2, all of the old feelings came back in spades. As the members encountered each difficult interpersonal situation, they would struggle with whether they wished to attempt to manage it on their own or whether they preferred to ask the former supervisor to intervene. This supervisor, now the team coach, did have the legitimate authority to intervene and was perfectly willing to do so. It was his belief that the women would not be able to manage such situations alone, so being called in to mediate met his expectations.

A human resources staff member assigned to support the development of the team was frequently consulted and consistently gave the same advice. The team could call on the supervisor to handle the situation, but it could not expect to grow as a team so long as it did so. The only way in which the team could develop and move forward was to struggle with these situations and resolve them without the supervisor's intervention. This was, of course, not what the team members wanted to hear. They believed that they could turn the tough stuff over to the former supervisor and still be a functional team performing the easier aspects of their jobs. It was made clear to the team members that the choice of how conflict was managed was solely within their control and that the consequences of the choices were theirs as well.

Tough situations continued to be deferred to the coach and, predictably, conflict worsened within the team. Finally, the members agreed to try to work through a conflict situation themselves, as a team, without the intervention of their coach. They struggled for some time, and tension within the team grew to almost unbearable heights. It seemed as though everyone's worst fears were realized. Then, a breakthrough came. Resolution was reached, and the team took a significant leap toward high performance.

They were still in Phase 2, and conflict did not magically disappear. However, team members learned two important lessons. First, they learned that they were capable of managing conflict on their own. Second, they learned that managing conflict on their own made them stronger and better able to handle conflict the next time it occurred. That awareness made them more open to differences of opinion, which, in turn, propelled them toward increasing levels of high performance.

mean being unconcerned or inattentive; it does mean pushing issues back to the team. If, for example, team meetings are criticized as being a waste of time, the team should be challenged to change them. It should not be someone else's job to make the team's meetings work, regardless of how much the team might try to make it so. If the meetings are not worthwhile, it must be pointed out that the team owns them and can make them more productive if it wishes to.

Phase 2 represents heightened sensitivity on the part of both Gen Xers and Baby Boomers. Boomers will often want to go back to whatever was working before someone decided this group should be a team. They will make efforts to refocus on their work and avoid anything that relates to building a team. Gen Xers will also withdraw. They don't want to spend their time in open conflict with older adults. Remember, too, that this is the generation that changes jobs frequently, so leaving is very much an option. Boomers are not inclined to physically walk away; they value loyalty to the company and following the direction of their formal leader. However, their behavior may be a fine example of "malicious compliance." Boomer withdrawal will be mental and spiritual; they will participate in the team in body only.

Phase 2 Strategies for Success

Unlike traditional team approaches that seek to resolve or avoid conflict, authentic teams seek to generate energy and creativity from the conflict that is inherent in all teams. Structure allows that to happen. In Phase 2, it is important to

- Continue to hold team meetings on a regular schedule and to require team members to attend. If the organization has adopted teams as its structure of choice, then team meetings are a part of what each person is being paid to do. Meetings must continue, and they must be mandatory. It is impossible to mandate *meaningful* participation, but disallow any behavior that would be unacceptable at the workstation. For example, if reading magazines or idle chatter is not appropriate at any other work setting, it should also be inappropriate at a team meeting.

- Continue to train as an intact team, and use real issues as the focus of conflict management and problem-solving training.

- Use what the team is experiencing as an opportunity to learn about individual team members and about the best dynamics for the team's effectiveness.

- Work on specific tasks for which the team is accountable: for example, customer service audits or cross-training in job skills.

The Gestalt value of being up-front plays heavily in Phase 2. Team members as individuals must be supported on issues that are important to them as individuals. The rule is that honesty prevails. While a team member chooses how much he or she discloses to the group, whatever is disclosed must be honest. This rule allows each individual to carve out a comfort zone within the conflict around him or her. By putting an individual stake in the ground around what is acceptable and what is not, each member in turn also makes a link to the team. This is how the unique identity of a team is formed. Phase 2 pushes team members to the edge and then gently delivers them into Phase 3.

Given the known difficulties of Phase 2, many teams seek to avoid it. They will demonstrate in Phase 1 what a good team they are and how they have been able to move into Phase 3 without the expected pain. And they may successfully postpone Phase 2 for a while. Performance of the group (it is still a group rather than a team) may even be slightly higher than it was before. However, the full potential of the individuals involved in a Phase 1 or 2 team does not come anywhere close to fulfillment.

The Use of Subteams and Games

One very successful technique in helping a team move through Phase 2 is to make regular use of subteams for various tasks or for games. Subteams differ from subgroups in that they are assigned; subgroups are self-selected groups of people who have aligned around common beliefs or positions. Subteams are more structured. They need to be established randomly by numbering, or alphabetically, or by whatever means will break up existent subgroups, and they need to be charged with a specific task. When the task is completed, new subteams are formed for the next task, and so on. Subteams established randomly (as opposed to subgroups in which individuals use inclusion and exclusion tactics) allow opposing team members to work together for a designated period.

Games are a particularly helpful activity during Phase 2. They allow people to talk to one another about something that does not constitute a threat, and they find that they can work effectively together in spite of their differences.

A typical game might involve unscrambling sets of letters into names of cities. Subteams are established, and each team is given the puzzle and a period of time in which to solve it. Points are awarded for each correct answer. Individual confidence builds as participants contribute to their subteams according to their personal knowledge and strength. The team member whose parents came from Texas, for example, may be able to identify El Paso among the mixed letters, while the team member from Missouri correctly identifies St. Louis. Collaboration also slips into the discussions as one person's guess triggers another person's identification of the city. The confidence that individuals experience in the games leads to greater willingness to participate in large team discussions and decisions.

Games do not need to take a large amount of meeting time (fifteen or twenty minutes is typical), and they do not need to be played often. They are, however, a valuable diversion periodically, as they generate multiple positive dynamics. First, people laugh together. Second, people interact with people they might never have chosen to interact with. Third, individuals find that they do have something to contribute, even if it is something quite different from what another team member can contribute.

The classroom experiment on the next page demonstrates how games can influence individual team member performance.

Generation X team members like games and will even like working within a subteam to accomplish tasks. In general, they are a gregarious bunch and prefer the social interaction that a small group offers. Boomers, on the other hand, are not at all comfortable with the notion of playing games when one is supposed to be working. It is during these small-group activities, however, that team members learn the capabilities and limits of their fellow team members. When the group is small, it is much more likely that there will be a sharing of personal information that contributes to the group's success.

*J*un, a Chinese student in a graduate-level team-building class, was very concerned about her ability to participate in class activities because her language skills were not as strong as she would have liked. She was very quiet, and fellow members of her in-class team, most of whom were competitive, aggressive, and very verbal, gave her little opportunity for input. After observing this behavior for three games in a row, the instructor introduced a game in which no team member could talk to another. All communication was to be nonverbal. Guess who took over and led her team to success? Jun gave directions and got input from other team members without having to compete in an arena in which she had felt handicapped. Other team members, recognizing her expertise in an area in which they had little experience, willingly followed her lead, and the team was successful in winning the game. In subsequent games, greater effort was made to seek the involvement of this quiet team member who had proven her value to the team effort.

Remember that in Phase 1, team members learned about the ways in which they were different. In Phase 2, they learn how to capitalize on those differences. It is here, too, that team members experience personal recognition and reward in the context of team success. This is a critical learning point for authentic teams: Each team member must come to know that he or she is a unique contributor to the team's success and that personal success is very much a part of overall team success.

Recognizing Transition to Phase 3

What helps push a team out of Phase 2 and into Phase 3 is individual awareness of one's value to the team. When each team member believes that he or she has something of value to contribute, and then takes the initiative to speak up and make that contribution while accepting the risk that others may disagree, the team's dynamics change.

Members of high-performing teams talk about their individual turning points, often without being aware of their significance to the team's overall performance. One team member described being put into a new team with members who had once been his managers but were now his peers. He described how the group had initially given more credence to opinions of their former managers, yet at the same time resented any behavior that indicated they were not equal participants. When this individual eventually realized that his input carried just as much weight as that of his former boss, the team began to work for him.

Another member of a Phase 3 team commented that she was very comfortable participating and even taking an active role on the team when she could do so in areas in which she knew her expertise was solid. It was her expectation that as her expertise grew, her involvement would expand.

How long it takes a team to work through Phase 2 varies from team to team. However, it is critical to realize that without proper support and understanding, a team can get stuck in Phase 2 and die. When it is too late to turn back to the way things were done before, and when going forward seems impossible, it is very likely that a Phase 2 team will go nowhere. One Phase 2 team in a manufacturing facility that was stuck for a period of years illustrates this dilemma.

The team membership at this manufacturing facility was remarkably stable, with no one leaving and no new members coming into the team. Team meetings were held on a weekly basis, and they were routine and boring. To compound the difficulty, team members didn't like one another. Reports were read, but there was little conversation and even less eye contact between members. The conflict was unspoken, yet the nonverbal signals of hostility at team meetings were hard to overlook.

The coach decided to give games a try after seeing the success other teams in the factory had experienced in using them. After all, he had little to lose. He assigned team members to subteams and challenged them with games he designed himself, using "Who Wants to Be a Millionaire?" as his source of team challenges. Teams accumulated points for correct answers, and points led to rewards at the end of each series of games. When a series ended and rewards were distributed, members were reassigned to new subteams and began another series of competitions.

Within two months of starting the games at weekly meetings, this team completed its Phase 2 assignments and moved into Phase 3. Team members began interacting comfortably, and the team started getting things done efficiently and effectively. The atmosphere at team meetings is now relaxed and cordial. One would think, by observing them together, that these team members have been functioning effectively as a team for a very long time.

It is *not* recommended that any team be allowed to struggle in Phase 2 for years; however, it is also unrealistic to expect each team to experience Phase 2 exactly the same way. Members of high-performing teams advise new teams to embrace the struggles of Phase 2 and use all of the tools and techniques described above to navigate it successfully. In fact, it is reasonable to assume that many of the team failures we hear about are actually a result of hitting Phase 2 and quitting when the going gets rough. Yet as the team moves into Phase 3, it is individual strength borne of the difficulty in Phase 2 that brings the team as a whole to high performance.

Indications that the team may be on its way into Phase 3 include

- Discussions are raised to a higher plane, with a focus on issues instead of personalities.

- Team members seek out action steps rather than just talking about what is wrong.

- Conflict still exists, but it has a very different tone. Opposing points of view are respected rather than rejected.

- Often at the end of Phase 2, a team member will choose to leave the team. It is important to let that person go, knowing that a team is not the right structure for everyone, and to view it as a success rather than a failure. When an individual acts from the strength of his or her convictions, and that decision is honored and respected by other members of the team, there has indeed been growth for all involved.

Individuals who survive Phase 2 together enter Phase 3 as a tight, sustainable, high-performing team. The effort each individual has exerted, willingly or otherwise, to get to this point constitutes a bond that is difficult to break. It is time to reap the rewards of Phase 3.

Phase 3: Norming

Entry into Phase 3 seems almost miraculous. As one coach described the transition of her team, "Yesterday, they hated each other; today, they're getting along great!" In Phase 3, behaviors become significantly different. The most obvious difference is that respect has replaced control. Instead of struggling over who is right and who is wrong, team members find themselves respecting each other's right to be different. Gestalt practice mandates that individuals be self-supportive and in control of their own lives and that they allow each other person to do the same. This individual independence, in conjunction with valuing each individual's uniqueness, lays the foundation for team "norming." In completing tasks assigned to the team, discussions center on (1) what has to be done; (2) who is best equipped to do it, better at doing it, or wants to learn to do it; and (3) how team members can support one another in getting it done. During Phase 3, individual team members utilize what they have learned about one another in a productive rather than judgmental way. The pressure of trying to conform and like one another is replaced with the comfort and flexibility of knowing each other "authentically."

Higher-order tasks are characteristic in Phase 3. Teams spend more time designing or redesigning their work processes to fit the needs of the organization as well as the needs of individual team members. Cross-training is initiated within the team in varying degrees of depth. Whereas the ideal team formerly consisted of a group of individuals equally skilled in all areas of team responsibility, that is no longer the norm. Increasingly, team members are recognizing that their self-esteem and productivity are enhanced when they consider themselves "experts" in something that represents a unique contribution to the team.

Consider the difference between the traditional team, where team members are encouraged to be interchangeable, and the authentic team, where each individual's expertise is acknowledged and celebrated as a team strength. Cross-training is still important, but the level to which all team members are trained is not as high as was once envisioned. Team members are trained to be able to back one another up and to understand the jobs that other members do and how they fit into the team's overall objectives. However, a backup is not expected to be an expert. Each team member becomes a "generalist" in the work of the team but retains a specific area of expertise that enhances the team's capabilities.

In Phase 3, team members are able to decide (1) the level of cross-training that makes sense to them in their environment, and (2) the best way to get everyone to the desired level of expertise. It is likely to take some time to accomplish initial cross-training goals, and cross-training is likely to continue throughout the life of the team in support of high performance. In Phase 3, team members are capable of designing a process that works best for them. Consider the following case.

A team of customer service representatives who handled a range of very complex and detailed products set up what they called a buddy system. Each representative became a backup for another representative—or became his or her buddy. Each became proficient enough to handle calls on the products handled by both partners. Once proficient in two products, buddies were reassigned, and each representative learned another product in order to serve as backup for his or her new buddy. The team determined that it would neither be possible nor in the interest of good customer service for each person to be equally proficient in all products; the products were just too complex for that goal to be realistic. However, a goal of cross-trained subunits of three to five people each was both realistic and attainable. What mattered most was that the participants took ownership of the process and made it work.

It is critical for a work team to integrate its team structure into its operational structure so that the two become seamless. Work teams that seem to float outside the flow of day-to-day operations can never be fully effective, high-performing teams. The team concept must be integrated as a way of life. One way in which this can often happen is through a change in team meeting format and function. For example, teams in Phase 3 will often institute daily "floor" meetings as a supplement to or in exchange for weekly meetings. A customer service team can institute daily 11 a.m. stand-up meetings in the department. Everyone gathers in a central place, team members comment on what demands they are facing for the day and, where appropriate, work is reassigned to enable the highest levels of effectiveness for the team. Similarly, manufacturing teams can schedule fifteen-minute meetings at the start of a shift, or at shift change, to share information and hand off work assignments to the appropriate team members. While such meetings may not seem remarkable, the important thing to remember is that team members, not supervisors, are driving these meetings, and work is being deployed without the involvement of a management representative. With daily meetings to address short-term work-related issues, weekly or biweekly meetings can then be focused on larger issues that require additional time for resolution.

Teams in Phase 3 will often revisit their initial guidelines to ensure they are still appropriate for how the team wishes to operate. If the guidelines are no longer relevant, the team will make adjustments to reflect what has been learned since Phase 1 tasks were accomplished. Many teams also revisit specific areas of initial team training because they find the lessons more meaningful in light of recent team experiences. Team members have commented that it is almost like entirely new training because of their change in perspective. In addition to these reviews, teams in Phase 3 may also undertake specific skill areas, such as budgeting or process improvement, or examine quality issues in greater depth. These activities serve to enhance the cohesion the team has reached in Phase 3 as well as acknowledge the value of continued team development. In Phase 3, the team is able to address both task and process development equally well and will successfully integrate team activities with work activities. The "either/or" mentality of Phases 1 and 2 does not carry into Phase 3.

Generation differences become team strengths in Phase 3. As team members become more confident, they become less critical of others. This in turn allows individuals to be more open to new experiences and more willing to say when something doesn't work for them. Because of the increased support exhibited by fellow team members, it is not unusual for a Baby Boomer member of a Phase 3 team to venture into a previously avoided task. The same is true for Gen Xers. Each becomes a teacher of the other, and each accepts that what works well for him or her might not work so well for someone else—and that's okay!

Phase 3 is where true synergy begins. The whole becomes greater than the sum of its parts. This is not the great melting pot of traditional teams; Phase 3 is an enlargement of the "capabilities pie" that permits unique individuals, working together, to create far more than any one individual could accomplish alone.

In Phase 3, the effort required to make the team work effectively diminishes dramatically, and performance levels skyrocket. Some teams remain in Phase 3 for a long time, and are able to return significant value to their organizations. In many situations, Phase 3 performance, which is characterized by the team taking more control over its day-to-day operational activities, is sufficient to meet the needs of the organization. Other teams, however, move quickly into the levels of high performance that are characteristic of a Phase 4 team. If the team must achieve challenging objectives, then the push for high performance emerges naturally in Phase 3. Being a high-performance team starts to feel like a natural state, and the dark days of Phase 2 are left well behind.

Phase 4: Performing

Phase 4 is known as the high-performance, or "performing" stage for teams. For authentic teams, Phase 4 represents a new environment in which each person is willing and able to contribute his or her best in the achievement of team objectives. The Gestalt values of individual autonomy and increased awareness of existing behaviors come to full flower in Phase 4. Individuals in Phase 4 teams are there because they choose to be there. Interviews with team members reveal that individual choice plays a key role in both individual and team success. Phase 4 team members express high levels of satisfaction with their teams and yet feel confident that similar levels of performance and satisfaction could be reached with another team, given the effort. While these individuals have little influence over the opinions of those still struggling in Phases 1 and 2, the sentiments of Phase 4 team members are remarkably consistent.

Perhaps the most remarkable attribute of Phase 4 team members is their ability to see each other as unique individuals without categorizing anyone by age, gender, race, or religion. No Gen Xer is determined to be of lesser value to the team by a Baby Boomer peer, or vice versa. Each is respected for his or her contribution to the team, period. If an individual is capable of making a contribution but chooses not to do so, that decision is honored as well. This is not to imply that there are no disagreements; conflict is actually quite high in a Phase 4 team. However, the conflict is always around issues. The purpose of the conflict is to find the best way to proceed, and everyone on the team knows that. Consensus, that magical state that eludes so many teams, happens regularly in Phase 4 teams. When the team reaches consensus it aligns around the decision and implements it to the best of its ability.

High-performing teams have long been characterized as having a "rhythm" to their operations. Observations of a real Phase 4 team illustrate this rhythm at work.

*A*t their weekly meeting, the room quickly fills with team members, laughing and talking among themselves. Each has come armed with notebook, pen, papers, and reports. There is easy chatter about who is in charge of the meeting and when the coach might be able to join them. The designated facilitator for the meeting, determined by a rotation schedules, starts the meeting by asking for standing reports that the team consistently has on the agenda: reports on production, safety, and quality. Other reports follow, and action items are wrapped up and reports are closed that were not resolved at the last meeting. If there is an open item to be discussed, an individual "sponsor" for that issue begins the discussion with an update and an indication of what the team needs to accomplish in order to bring the issue to closure.

During discussions, a sort of ordered chaos occurs. Each person is encouraged to express an opinion—and to ensure that his or her position has been properly represented to the group. Quiet members are encouraged to participate or are at least asked for an opinion. More vocal members are encouraged to give airtime to those less aggressive individuals who are at risk of being shut out. While the facilitator might inject some guidance, the team is largely self-facilitated. Discussion continues until some action is agreed on, whether that action is to collect more information, table the issue until the next meeting, or reach a resolution. A timekeeper is often employed to ensure that no one discussion goes too long and prevents other items from being discussed.

Individual team members introduce new items; discussion again follows, concluding in action plans for various members of the team. The meeting has defined time boundaries and, as the time runs out, the facilitator checks with other team members to determine how any remaining agenda items are to be handled. Options are to appoint subteams to work on issues and report back to the next meeting or to table items for discussion by the whole team next time. Running over the designated time allotment is rarely an option. The meeting adjourns on time, and each team member goes back to work.

Back on the job, a different kind of rhythm sets in. Each team member knows what has to be done and knows his or her role in getting it done. No one has to direct anyone else; each person takes the initiative to meet his or her own responsibilities. Periodic checks with each other ensure that everyone is aware of progress against goals. If anyone encounters a problem, the team will be brought together for assistance or an individual team member will be sought out for expertise or advice.

Every individual on an authentic team is a confident contributor and is willing to say when and if help is needed. Each member takes pride in the team's achievements. Each member will go to the aid of any other member if and when aid is needed and knows that the favor will be returned. There are disagreements, and there is conflict, but they are never personal. Disagreements and conflict are used to make a team stronger, and team members take them as a matter of course.

Casual observers of a Phase 4 team might miss the significance of its interactions, so integrated are the interactions into the flow of the workday. Team members themselves, in fact, often take their performance for granted. If they step back and assess where they are compared to where they have been in the past, then progress and performance seem astounding. Perhaps even more astounding is the realization that this level of high performance has become a way of life, and no one on the team can imagine working any other way.

Teams in Phase 3 and in Phase 4 produce high quality and high quantity, and enjoy what they are doing. Documented achievements include

- One team realized production yield above goal for fourteen straight weeks.

- Another team achieved a significant reduction of customer complaints.

- A Phase 3 team increased first-time test yield from 92.2 percent to 94.03 percent in a one-year period.

- Cycle count adjustments in a Phase 4 team went from $197,000 to $39,000 in one year.

- Productivity in another team increased by 34 percent in one year.

- On-time delivery performance was held at 100 percent for thirteen weeks straight by yet another high-performing team.

Team members also cite qualitative improvements in their operations, including increased communication and information sharing among team members, and a greater awareness of the "big picture." Other teams cite a better understanding of how individual contributions affect the group or the company, an outcome that supports teams as a valid structure for the Baby Boomer/Generation X mix. Finally, team members report an increased level of buy-in because team members make most decisions that affect their team. With buy-in and ownership comes a more positive outcome for everyone involved.

For a high-performing team, there is no difference in value between a Baby Boomer team member, a Gen X team member, or any other team member, regardless of the generation of which he or she is a member. Workers respect themselves, each other, and their organization and focus their energy on making their work the best it can possibly be.

Authentic teams are simple, but they are definitely not easy. This chapter and the matrix in Appendix B give you the context and content for building authentic teams. In the following chapter, we will expand on a critical role in this process, the role of the coach. We will also discuss how to bring new members into a Phase 4 team and how to extend high-performance work teams to a high-performance organization.

CHAPTER 4

Supporting Authentic Teams

Building authentic teams is only the beginning. Authentic teams must be supported by the organization and its structures if high performance is to endure. Much has been written about the importance of using teams only for interdependent tasks that can benefit from a team structure. We agree that to attempt to install teams where such interdependence is not required is to waste time and effort for all involved. The nature of the work must lend itself to a need for people to interact effectively, or there is no need for a team. Effective interaction brings synergy, the phenomenon where the sum of the parts is greater than the whole. Synergy can only happen when two or more people are involved.

Recognition and reward for team effort and success are also critical; however, common sense is encouraged. If authentic teams celebrate both the team and the individual team member as integral to organizational success, then rewards should mirror this structure. Rewards for authentic teams should reflect individual achievement, team achievement, and organizational achievement, in an appropriate balance for the situation involved. What is important is that all three are considered when rewards are made.

If a team is properly developed, supported by the organization's structure, and rewarded for its achievements, little else is needed for ongoing success. However, two crucial factors are often given too little attention in building effective teams. They are the role of the coach and the management of changing membership in an ongoing team.

The Coach

In their younger days, many Baby Boomers defied authority. As teenagers, Boomers wanted a voice and wanted to have choices about every aspect of their lives. Over time, most came to accept that having a boss was their destiny. For Boomers, bosses were older folks who had been in the workforce for a while and knew how the game of work was played. Bosses were the Boomers' parents.

The world of work for Gen Xers is somewhat different. Xers listened to their parents talk of freedom at work and at home, of what they would do when they were able to be in charge, and of the great ideas they had for improving their work lives, if only anyone would listen. Xers listened, and they vowed to have the voice that their parents longed for. Thus, as more and more Gen Xers enter the workplace, the traditional role of boss is being pushed out of the way. Empowerment, autonomy, and self-direction are all important to Xers, and those elements defy the traditional definition of "boss."

The workplace is still very much in a state of transition. A future generation may be able to enter a fully self-managed workplace as a matter of course, and not a single ripple will be felt. However, we aren't there yet. While the mix of generations at work remains heavily weighted with Boomer workers, the role of boss must still be addressed. In the world of work teams, that boss becomes the coach.

Every team needs a coach, someone to help guide it through the trials of working effectively together to achieve success. A coach is a given in most sports settings. Can you imagine a high-performing sports team without an effective coach? Highly publicized searches for the right coach keep teams at high-performance levels. Why would we place less importance on the coaches who manage our organizational teams?

In many organizations, the coach, or the individual responsible for a given team's development and performance, is not a true coach at all.

Instead, the person who wears the coach's hat is all too often a former supervisor whose old job was eliminated with the introduction of teams. It's not too hard to imagine the kinds of emotional baggage one might bring to the new role under these circumstances. Add to this the reality that many of these coaches are provided with little or no support or development. They are rarely given an opportunity to create a vision of what their jobs will be when the team no longer needs them, yet they are charged with the development of a team that will no longer need them at some point.

Among those who research team performance, the jury is still out on the importance of the coach's role. Manz and Sims (1987) found the behavior of individuals they identified as "coordinators" of teams to be critical to team development. These coordinators would parallel the coach in team-based organizations today. Manz and Sims found that the most relevant coaching behaviors for the support of self-managed teams were (1) the encouragement of self-reinforcement and (2) the encouragement of self-observation and evaluation. Coaches encouraged self-reinforcement by continually pointing out to team members what they were doing well. Coaches also encouraged team members to be increasingly aware of their own actions and the effect those actions had on work situations. In this way, team members could learn from each experience and improve their behavior the next time a similar situation arose. These supporting behaviors by coaches allowed team members to develop to desired levels of high performance.

More recently, in a comprehensive review of literature about what makes teams work in organizational settings, Cohen and Bailey (1997) found encouraging supervisory behavior to be a negative predictor of performance for self-directed work groups. This finding is in direct contradiction to the findings of Manz and Sims.

Forces at Work

Two models are helpful in understanding the appropriate role of a coach in the development and ongoing support of authentic teams. Tannenbaum and Schmidt (1958) developed a continuum of leadership behavior that encouraged a leader to choose the degree of authority given to subordinates according to the ability of subordinates to make effective decisions on their own. The authors urged managers to take into consideration three "forces" in the organizational environment: (1) forces in the leader, (2) forces in subordinates, and (3) the nature of the situation.

Forces in the leader include

- His or her value system

- His or her strength of conviction that individuals should have a share in making decisions that affect them

- His or her confidence in subordinates and their ability to make good decisions

- His or her leadership inclinations and preferences with regard to decision making

- His or her tolerance for ambiguity and ability to allow control of the situation to be in the hands of others

Forces in the subordinate include

- Their need for independence

- Their readiness to assume responsibility for decision making

- Their tolerance for ambiguity or their requirements for clear-cut direction from others

- Their ability to understand and identify with the goals of the organization

- Their level of knowledge and experience to deal with the problem

- Their expectation to share in decision making

Forces in the situation include

- The nature of the problem itself

- The time available to make a decision

- The effectiveness of group members' work together

- The values and traditions of the organization in similar situations

• The long-term strategy of the organization with regard to how much decision-making authority subordinates are to be given in the future

In a 1973 retrospective commentary, Tannenbaum and Schmidt added two more dimensions for consideration. One was the degree of interdependency of the original forces. The forces themselves do not function in isolation from one another, but rather create a dynamic that must be taken into consideration in determining where the best decisions lie. The second dimension, already obvious in 1973, was the changing nature of workers. Tannenbaum and Schmidt reflected on workers who resent being treated like subordinates and who expect to be consulted and to exert influence. Certainly today these factors are even more critical than they were in 1973.

Tannenbaum and Schmidt's notion of how to manage shared decision making is still solid and resounds with common sense. Decision-making authority is best handled by those who have the knowledge, skills, and experience to make good decisions, and those people are not always the managers.

Tannenbaum and Schmidt's concepts were popularized in 1969 by Paul Hersey and Ken Blanchard in their book *Management of Organizational Behavior: Utilizing Human Resources*. Popularly known as "situational leadership," Hersey and Blanchard's model, too, discusses a gradual transition of power from manager to subordinate according to the subordinate's ability and desire to accept authority. Hersey and Blanchard further suggest that, at the individual level, the ability and/or desire may fluctuate from one day to the next and from one situation to the next. As such, it is the manager's responsibility to assess the individual's or the team's capacity to handle a decision at a given point and to develop decision-making capacity over time. Development is accomplished through the use of successive approximations, or "baby steps" in decision making that teach, support, and encourage the individual and the team to take on increasingly difficult decisions as they become capable of handling them.

Both models, Tannenbaum and Schmidt's as well as Hersey and Blanchard's, have withstood the test of time. They suggest that the person in authority in most team-based organizations makes power and authority available to individuals and teams only when they are ready to handle them. When one is new to the job, or new to the team, he or she will be given less decision-making authority because the knowledge and experience on which to base a sound decision are not yet developed. Conversely, in a mature team, significant levels of power and authority can be shared because the team is capable of making sound decisions.

The Role of the Coach

The role of the coach is critical in the early stages of team development and becomes less important as the team matures. Indeed, some models have the coach evolving back into the team as an equal member when the team is fully developed. Observations of high-performing teams support the position of coach as equal team member, with the exception of designated functions such as firing and salary administration, or whatever else corporate policy prevents team members from doing for themselves. In a union environment, such boundaries may be prescribed by the union's contract with management.

It is unlikely a team will reach levels of high performance without the support and direction of a strong coach in the early stages of its development. Consider, for example, in the story on the next page, two teams in the same organization, each working on similar products and with similar clients, each having similar characteristics among its members with regard to age, gender, education, experience levels, and time with the company.

Two lessons can be learned from the experiences of these contrasting teams. First, it is important that the coach knows what he or she is doing in terms of both the job and the team. Train the coach first. Give the coach the tools needed to teach and develop the team. Reward the coach for development of the team, and offer the coach a clear vision of how his or her time will be spent when the team is more self-sufficient. Encourage the coach to work himself or herself out of a job so that a more exciting job can be explored. In other words, teach the coach to be a coach, then reward the coach for coaching.

Second, the team's struggle to become high-performing can stretch on endlessly if there is no impetus for change. The coach must be willing to step into the fray and learn along with the team about what works best. Coaching, in the case of teams, is a hands-on job for the first two stages. Then, as individual team members become more knowledgeable

*T*he most striking difference between these two teams was found in their respective coaches. One coach was very strong, with a dominant style, very well versed in the business for which he was accountable, and very successful in his performance prior to the establishment of teams. The other was less experienced, more relaxed by nature, less demanding of his direct reports, and not as confident in his ability to lead. Over a two-year development period, the first coach, who had made it clear that when his team became more self-managing he would be free to do other, more attractive work, took his team to the point of being the highest-performing self-managed team in the organization. Within those same two years, the coach of the other team was unable to move his team out of Phase 1. There were some obvious differences in the styles of these coaches and the ways in which they developed and supported their teams.

The first coach, Bill, had great confidence in himself and in his people. He had previously taught them their business well, and he approached teaching them as a team with the same vigor. They were encouraged to make decisions, challenged to improve their performance, and provided with all the support and attention they needed to do both. Bill stayed and struggled with his team as it went through the difficult phases of its development. This included periods when the members did not want him present at meetings, periods when they wanted him there to make decisions so they wouldn't have to, and periods when they were angry at him for making decisions they had wanted to make for themselves. Over time Bill came to trust team members, team members came to trust themselves, and Bill turned over nearly all day-to-day operational decisions to the team.

The coach of the other team, Tom, took a different tack. He was a relatively new manager, having become a supervisor just prior to the introduction of teams. He was less experienced in the business and knew less about its products and customers than did Bill. Tom's response to the introduction of self-managed teams was to abdicate all authority. This was followed by periods when he allowed no decisions by the team, primarily because he had little confidence in its decision-making ability, followed closely by periods when he abdicated authority again. This pattern continued for most of the team's two years together. The team did not develop, learn, or grow. Neither did Tom. Tom's continued fluctuations between loose and tight management inspired no confidence in his perception of the team's capabilities. The team, likewise, was not confident of Tom's capabilities. This team remained stuck throughout the two-year period that it was under observation.

and confident in themselves and each other, more delegation to the team is possible. Becoming a high-performing team requires an evolution, not a revolution, if high performance is to be achieved and sustained.

In an authentic team, individual strengths of team members and of the coach work together to become the strength of the team. It is combined strength and the ongoing cultivation of that strength that sustains high performance over time. The coach is, as Manz and Sims (1987) suspected, critical to the team's success, but primarily in the early stages (Phases 1 and 2) rather than in stages of high performance. As Cohen and Bailey (1997) found, too much attention by the coach can be a negative force, particularly when the team is in Phases 3 and 4. Successful development of a high-performance work team requires a coach who is willing to abide by concepts set forth by Tannenbaum and Schmidt and by Hersey and Blanchard: The coach must coach the team.

Team Member Changes

One fact we have stressed throughout this book is that nothing stays the same for very long in today's organizations. This great source of frustration for many Boomers is a wellspring of excitement for many Xers. And it creates a problem for team development as we have known it in the past.

In 1957, R. B. Cattell introduced the term *syntality*. In its most basic form, syntality is to a group what personality is to the individual. Assumptions about syntality are important considerations when looking at the life of a team. Whether a team is formed under the values and strategies implicit in the traditional model or under those implicit in the authentic model will greatly influence that team's stability and long-term effectiveness.

Traditional models of group development suggest that a group will undergo dramatic changes when there are changes in membership. The idea that the team will return to its developmental infancy with the introduction of a new personality makes logical sense in that a whole new set of dynamics is introduced in the person of the new member. This notion has caused great frustration among the work teams of today's rapidly changing business environment. In the days when workers stayed with one company and in one job, life was predictable, and it was considered a sign of success to be with one employer for one's entire work history. In these circumstances, the notion of a work group that changed little made sense, and the trauma of change loomed high on the list of things to be avoided.

Today's world is different. Not only do younger workers measure job tenure in increments of three to five years, but older workers can no longer count on the lifelong security their employers once provided. Companies change, work changes, people come and go. To suggest, or expect, that a work team will remain intact over any significant period of time is to indulge in fantasy. Under traditional concepts of group development, the changing dynamics of today's workforce suggest that long-term success for any work group or team is unlikely. If the team must redevelop from scratch each time a new person enters the team, then work life becomes an endless cycle of team training. And, in many organizations, that is exactly what has happened.

Traditional team development processes call for a team to revisit its mission and guidelines with the entry of each new member. This became a real problem for second- and third-shift teams in the manufacturing facility we introduced in chapter 1.

The typical process of employment in this facility was to start as a third-shift worker, then bid for positions on second and then first shifts as they became available. This assumed, of course, that the employee did not leave the company before becoming eligible to bid for another shift. As a result, the churn on third shift was constant, and it was also problematic on second shift. First-shift teams were more stable, and eventually developmental efforts strayed away from the off-shift teams and became concentrated on first shift.

During one unexpected period of relative stability, a third-shift team determined that it would complete the team development process and achieve Phase 4. It worked diligently to accomplish the required training, and over a period of about six months met all of the requirements of a Phase 4 team. The team mirrored other teams in the facility in terms of age and gender mix, but, of course, it had members with less seniority than did most first-shift teams. However, by the time it achieved Phase 4 status, this team exhibited all of the same behaviors as those routinely exhibited by Phase 4 teams in other parts of the organization. This team realized the success and high performance of a well-developed team.

Then, predictably, the stability ended and the churn began. Some members of the team had experienced earlier cycles of training and retraining, and, when new members were added, they flatly refused to do it again. They also refused to lose the progress they had made as a team. Instead, they found a better way to manage the change in membership. They decided that, from that point forward, when a new member joined the team, he or she would be brought up to where the team was rather than the team returning to Phase 1.

Each new member was given a team mentor, a senior member of the team who taught, supported, and coached the new member into a full-fledged, fully participating member of the team. New members were encouraged to take active roles in team activities. Other team members asked them for their opinions, gave them support in learning new job skills, and encouraged them to ask questions. New team members felt valued, and they quickly became equal members of their new, high-performing team.

The model of team development used here is consistent with the values of authentic management. When the group consistently values the uniqueness and independence of each of its members, it is easier to integrate a newcomer into an existing structure without disturbing the group's stability. So long as the team values differentiation as the necessary precursor of integration, it doesn't matter at what point in the team's life a change in membership occurs.

The experience of the team in this example provides an important lesson for any organization experiencing turnover and trying to support self-managed teams. While it has always been important for work groups to support and teach new co-workers, it is critical for members of high-performing teams to actively bring new members into the team in a way that sustains rather than undermines high performance.

Another lesson to take from the experience of this third-shift team is that a team must be willing to do whatever it takes to continue working in a successful way. While structure is important in the early stages of team development, structure often changes once the team reaches the high-performance stage. Such changes are appropriate at that point because by then the team is well aware of what is required to enable it to perform at its best. An example of a change commonly seen when a team becomes high-performing is a restructuring of team meeting times and agendas.

In any case, it is safe to assume that no two high-performing teams will behave in exactly the same way because a team cannot be successful without reflecting the uniqueness of its situational needs and its individual members.

Biography of a High-Performing, Self-Managed Team

In this section we look more closely at the remarkable success of the third-shift team, with a focus on how the team's coach helped it achieve Phase 4 performance. Names have been changed, but situations have not.

Pre-Team

They worked at night, starting at 11 p.m., about the time most people were going to bed. They ended their workday at 7 a.m., when others were just thinking about starting their day. It was a small group of ten people, and about as varied as a group could be: There were men and women in ages ranging from the mid-twenties to early fifties; some were single, some were married; some had children, others did not. Hispanic workers brought an ethnic mix to the group. Some people worked the night shift because they wanted to be home with young children during the day and save the cost of child care. Others went to school during the day and worked nights to help make ends meet and to take advantage of company-paid tuition. Some were there because they were new to the company and third shift was where a new person started. And some were there simply because they liked third shift, where things were more relaxed and the stress level was lower. Several members of the group had been on third shift for a long time and had no desire to change.

This third-shift manufacturing team, though part of a professed team-based organization, had experienced little in the way of formal team activity. Those who had been in the department when teams were first instituted had participated in initial team training; however, the rate of turnover on third shift made it difficult to build a team. Few members of the group had more than a passing acquaintance with some of their co-workers before someone moved on, either to another shift or to another company. Then, the third shift got Chris.

Christine Sandover had worked in the same manufacturing area on the same product line during first shift. The assignment to third shift was her first supervisory position. Chris was known to be a good worker, was respected as someone who knew the job well, and was generally well liked. She was also willing to take on supervision of a night shift, which not too many people had an interest in doing. In fact, she was determined to make her team the best team in the facility. Chris took her role as coach seriously.

Phase 1

Sunday night was the beginning of the team's work week. Chris instituted weekly team meetings every Sunday from 11 p.m. until midnight. This made sense because the machinery had not yet been started following the weekend break. Once started, the machinery needed to be manned continuously, so a team meeting that included everyone could be held only at the start of shift on Sunday nights. Meetings became a weekly institution. This is not to say that team members looked forward to them with great anticipation. The meetings were annoying to people who were tired from a weekend of regular hours and now faced a work week of nights. Team members were often sullen and showed little interest in interacting with one another. The few who tried to make the meetings fun found themselves expending more than their fair share of energy. It became a tradition to bring food in an attempt to instill a party atmosphere, and over time food came to be a catalyst for team interaction.

In the early stages, however, people communicated very little. They were not rude to one another, just uninvolved. It was clear that the team meeting was meant to satisfy Chris, and the members had no real desire to move beyond this requirement.

Chris dealt with members of her team in ways that mirrored the Gestalt values of an authentic team. She knew, intuitively, that the mind and body are integrated, so she encouraged team members to pay attention to both. Team members were not chastised for being tired; rather, their physical states were incorporated into discussions and team activities as another facet of what the team had to deal with. Chris was also consistent in her reminders to team members that personal choices were behind their physical well-being and that they had the right to make different choices if they wished. This was never done in a judgmental or demeaning way; rather, it was an acknowledgment of the adult status of each team member, regardless of age or time with the company.

Another value fostered by Chris from the beginning of her work on third shift was the conviction that good working relationships are the result of doing good work together. Chris pushed her team members hard. She pushed them to improve quality, increase output, and challenge their own best records. Putting good work ahead of good working relationships, in terms of which occurs first, is diametrically opposite to the way most teams attempt to work. Chris was very clear with her team that members did not have to like each other. All that was required was that they find a way to work together so that performance would reflect the talent within the team. Chris believed, and was proven correct, that if good work was accomplished, good relationships would follow.

The company's criteria for a Phase 1 team included a significant amount of training and the completion of a Phase 1 task checklist. A few team members had been through team training before, and they did not want to go through it again. Others were really not interested in having anything to do with teams, including untold hours of training. Some would do whatever they were told to do; if the company wanted to pay them to be in a class, it was fine with them. So training was scheduled in small increments of time over several months. Facilitated by an internal organization development specialist, it usually occurred on Thursday nights, after the week's production needs had been met. Classes typically lasted four hours, although one marathon eight-hour class was required to complete Phase 3 requirements

Team training included establishing the team's mission and guidelines. Boundaries for decision making were established between team and coach, and "star-point" coordinators were identified. A star-point coordinator was a team member responsible for keeping the team up to date in an assigned area of work. There were star-point coordinators for production, safety, and quality. An additional star-point coordinator was named to be in charge of social events, including the frequent potlucks and treats enjoyed during team meetings.

Chris attended every training session with her team, in addition to receiving special training for her role as coach in classes held during the day. It was not unusual to see Chris at an 8 a.m. class, working to satisfy her own credentials. Chris also attended every team meeting, ensuring that the team set an agenda and then followed it. When team members groaned about having to attend yet another meeting, or suggested that the meeting be cancelled, Chris reminded them of the company's mandate to be a team-based organization. Her advice to the members was that they make the most of the time scheduled for meetings; since they had to be there anyway, they might as well make it worthwhile.

Chris used the team meeting to share important information about the work the team was doing and to encourage ongoing team development. She commented on positive member behavior and reminded individuals that their behaviors, good or bad, could significantly affect their teammates. Standards of performance for the team were set, and team members were expected to meet them. If help was needed, it was readily supplied. If a team member did not know how to do a job that needed to be done, Chris or another team member would show him or her how. If team members dozed off at their workstations, Chris was nearby with her coach's whistle to remind them that they were at work. Team members were repeatedly reminded that only they could determine what they would do next and how they would do it.

As time went on, benign indifference gave way to more open resistance, and it became more difficult to coerce the team into participating in required team activities. What had seemed a novel idea initially, something that could be attributed to a new, enthusiastic coach, quickly became tiresome. Resistance surfaced in many forms, including open conflict between team members and refusal to perform roles assigned at the time the team began. Chris's team gradually but steadily moved into the dysfunction of Phase 2.

Phase 2

Looking back on this team's experiences in Phase 2, it is a wonder it survived at all. Chris's determination got the team through. She repeatedly reminded members that the team was not an option, that it was a requirement made by the company for all of its employees. When team members complained about meetings being a waste of time, Chris reminded them that the meetings were theirs and, if time was being wasted, it was up to them to do something about it. The team would meet for one hour every Sunday night, without fail. Other tasks might be shuffled to fulfill production schedules, but meetings were inviolate.

Those Sunday night meetings were not much fun; tempers flared, personal insults flourished, subgroups fought other subgroups, and some people stopped speaking to others altogether. Repeatedly, the coach reminded team members that their personal behavior was their personal responsibility. She also reinforced the idea that differences of opinion could enhance the team's performance if they were managed appropriately.

On the job, teaming was no more popular than it was in the meetings. People did not voluntarily help one another; they were told what to do by Chris, and there was no opportunity to resist. Later, Chris would point out to them the good work they had done together. And she refused to listen to their complaints. She simply said, "I don't want to hear it. You have a job to do; now, go do it."

Many mornings on her way out the door, Chris would shake her head in disbelief over how difficult her team had become. She was sure the members hated each other, had hated each other for a long time, and would hate each other forevermore. But, still, she persevered. Consistent with the values of authentic management, Chris was free to make demands for team interaction, and the team was free not to like it.

Chris's performance as a coach during Phase 2 was amazing. She never gave up on the team. She continually worked with team members, individually and as a group, to point out what they were doing well and to encourage them to try for more. When what they did caused problems, she was quick to make a link between individual choices and consequences, and she assured those involved that the outcome would be better when their choices were better. Chris was honest and fair with members of her team. She did not judge or play favorites. She encouraged people to use their strengths and encouraged the team to celebrate them. Although each member had weaknesses, they were acknowledged and managed in the best way possible. Each team member was treated with respect by the coach and, over time, by the other members.

One morning, Chris stopped by to announce to her organization development specialist that something had changed for the team. She wasn't sure what had happened, but she knew, as she put it, that "They went home last night hating each other and came back tonight getting along just fine." It was hard to describe, but Chris knew that a significant passage had been made. What the organization development specialist suspected was that Chris's team was ready to move into Phase 3.

Phase 3

The organization's requirements for a team to officially reach Phase 3 included completing all items on a Phase 2 checklist while continuing to practice all items on the Phase 1 checklist. The items were not easy to do and required cooperation to accomplish. One item on the checklist required the team to periodically review how well members were working together as a team and to make improvements where needed. Another required the team to identify key quality measures for its products, regularly collect data, analyze results, and implement changes to maintain or improve quality. There were twelve items on the Phase 1 checklist and fourteen on the Phase 2 list. Chris followed the team guidelines closely and made sure that no checklist items were overlooked. Such adherence to the standards set for all teams in the organization allowed Chris's team to transcend difficult interpersonal issues and enter into Phase 3.

After Chris's team made its transition into Phase 3, it immediately went to work on the checklist for Phase 3. Within about four weeks, it was ready to move into Phase 4. There were training recommendations for teams in Phases 2 and 3, and Chris's team completed them all. The workload was slow enough to allow one all-night, marathon training session with the whole team. These eight hours of training allowed the team to move, officially, into Phase 4. This third-shift team was the first manufacturing team in the facility to achieve Phase 4.

Phase 4

When the team reached Phase 4, a formal assessment was done to track its progress in mission, roles, and guidelines; teamwork; customer satisfaction; empowerment; and continuous improvement. The team also assessed the coach's performance. Assessment areas included planning and goal setting, coaching and guiding, empowering, monitoring team performance, developing and counseling, and supporting the team. Items in each category were rated on a scale of 1 (low) to 5 (high).

Average scores on the team assessment were all 3.5 or higher; on the coaching assessment, the lowest average score was 3.4.

Assessments also required that a team meeting be observed by an organization development specialist. There had been numerous observations of team meetings prior to that point, but none in an official capacity. The change in this team's Phase 4 meeting was striking. Chris sat in the back of the room, quietly, as the team's facilitator got the meeting started. By this time, several different team members had served as facilitator, so everyone was pretty familiar with what it took to be in the role and was careful to support whomever was currently taking a turn. Various star-point coordinators presented reports on their areas of focus, and discussion about each topic flowed easily and comfortably. Everyone participated. Conversation was fluid, with a lot of give-and-take.

While team members participated differently, depending on their own style and knowledge of the topic under discussion, there were no slackers on the team. Those who did not talk listened attentively. Discussions were supplemented by cheerful banter between team members, lightening the mood throughout the meeting. The diversity of the group became a source of teasing and joking, but always in a very positive and supportive manner. Meaningful discussions of work-related problems and solutions took place efficiently and effectively. Chris either was asked for information or volunteered it if she knew something about the topic under discussion that others did not. Her role in the meeting was one of equal team member, equal participant, one whose opinion carried the same weight as everyone else's. Chris still, however, had formal authority in certain areas. Because this was a union facility, contract boundaries were clear. The team was prohibited from making any decisions related to hiring, firing, or discipline of team members; those were Chris's responsibility. However, team members did have control over almost everything else related to their work life, and the decisions they made as a team were sound business decisions.

Documentation of the team's performance demonstrated a significant number of job certifications among team members, a goal for the entire manufacturing facility and one not easy to achieve on the off-shifts, when engineers and technical trainers are not readily available. Quality for the team's primary customer had improved significantly. More important, production rates had been maintained over a period of a year, resulting in a 99.0 percent yield rate. Another measure of productivity, the quantity of material produced by each person, had improved more than 400 percent. Past-due shipments had become a thing of the past as the team consistently met its weekly production goals. Interviews with team members showed similar positive improvements:

- "We have a laid-back environment where no one hounds you. They don't treat you like a kid. Work gets done a lot easier and faster than it used to."

- "We respect each other. We give each other good and constructive feedback. We have learned to give it and to receive it."

- "Emphasis on customer satisfaction is very high. Everyone shares the responsibility for mistakes, and we learn from them."

- "The coach tells us during a team meeting at the start of the shift what has to be done that night. Then we just do it. She gives us the priorities, and we decide who will do what."

- "We still have conflict, but we work it through. Our focus is on the work."

- "Chris challenges the team to do more all the time. You have a good feeling at the end of the day."

- "I like being on a team better than being an individual worker. This job requires people to work together effectively. I have learned to let other things go."

The real testament to this team's success came when activity at the plant slowed to a point where three shifts were no longer needed. In every other area of the facility, third-shift operations were shut down. It would have made sense to shut down Chris's team as well, to turn off the lights, turn down the heat, and keep the facility closed from the time second shift ended at 11 p.m. until first shift started up again at 7 a.m. the next day. It would have made sense, that is, if the performance of Chris's team had not been so exceptional. But the team's performance was so outstanding that it was allowed to continue to operate, and the second-shift operation for this area was shut down instead. This small team, less than half the size of the teams on first shift and second shift, outperformed its peers and, as a result, controlled its own destiny. This team was allowed to continue while others were cut back or eliminated altogether.

Epilogue

In the year since second shift was shut down, much has happened. Chris's team remains the only team on third shift, but a second-shift team is slowly rebuilding as product demand increases. Many who were members of the third-shift team when it achieved Phase 4 have since moved on to other shifts. In nearly every case, these former Phase 4 team members have taken steps to get their new teams on track and moving forward. They have become self-professed experts on how to make teams work, and they are anxious to recreate the experience they had as a member of Chris's team. Chris's team, with Chris still at the helm, continues to function as a Phase 4 team in spite of new members who now outnumber the original crew. New members have been mentored into the team and have quickly assumed active roles. Chris's team remains one of the most diverse in the facility and one of the most effective. And Chris, with her whistle, continues to be one of the best coaches around.

Christine Sandover did not have this book to follow as she developed her team. She did have, however, the full resources of a team-based organization, her own value system, and a lot of common sense. She put those things together to create a model for building authentic teams that exemplifies the concepts of individual collectivism we have discussed here. Individual members of Chris's team each make a unique contribution that collectively creates and sustains high performance. Every member of Chris's team, regardless of age, gender, or ethnicity, is important to the team's success. This is what authentic teams are all about—real people doing real work that benefits them and the company for which they work. It's not easy, but it is definitely possible.

CHAPTER 5

The Authentic Approach to Problem Solving

*T*he authentic model introduced in chapter 3 offers a breakthrough alternative to managing intergenerational teams, and it requires appropriate tactical tools to back up its successful implementation. Problem-solving tools in sync with the authentic model can diagnose individual needs and concerns of team members and establish appropriate links with team goals.

There are several problem-solving strategies that amply support the authentic model. A relatively new strategy originates from the body of knowledge known as "Theory of Constraints." In this chapter, a problem-solving tool called the "prerequisite tree," which is taken from Theory of Constraints, is presented along with two case studies.

Theory of Constraints

Theory of Constraints is a management philosophy developed by Eli Goldratt (1994). One of its basic principles is that the number of variables, or constraints, preventing a system from achieving its goals is very small. Most systems are composed of interrelated, interdependent links working together to achieve a predetermined goal. Intervening in one link may or may not affect the whole system, depending on how these interdependencies are built. In order to be stable, systems must have very few leverage points; otherwise, chaos will occur. The aim is to construct system descriptions in such a way that it is possible to determine key leverage points and types of interventions needed to obtain a desired result.

At the heart of Theory of Constraints is a set of logical tools known as the "thinking processes." These tools are based on strict logical procedure and have been used in myriad business applications. Thinking processes tools can be used to improve a system in diagnosing and developing directions and finding specific plans. Specific details about these tools are beyond the scope of this book; however, the process used to construct them is available in specialized books (see Dettmer 1997).

One of the most important premises of Theory of Constraints is that a system's behavior is governed by an underlying conflict. All undesirable effects observed in a system are the result of compromises adopted to manage the conflict. Team dynamics are no exception. If problems are encountered in teams, it is very likely that some fundamental conflict has not been resolved. In the case of intergenerational teams, our research shows that managing Gen Xers must take into account that they are both highly individualistic and highly team-oriented. Managing this apparent paradox requires innovative problem-solving skills.

Within Theory of Constraints, a prerequisite tree is a tactical tool used to plan the execution of an agreed-on objective. Its construction starts with determining the individual concerns of the members of the team, and only then trying to link those needs to the "ambitious target" of the team. What makes the prerequisite tree the technique of choice in problem solving with intergenerational teams is its insistence on airing all individual resistance as an essential step in achieving team objectives. Taking time to uncover individual resistance aligns these techniques with the authentic model.

Constructing a prerequisite tree consists of six steps.

1. Define the team's goal.

2. List obstacles to implementing the goal.

3. Determine intermediate objectives to overcome obstacles.

4. Map the implementation sequence of the intermediate objectives.

5. Assign intermediate objectives to team members.

6. Execute implementation plan.

After examining the six steps in detail, we will consider two case studies.

Building a Prerequisite Tree

1. DEFINE THE TEAM'S GOAL.

This step ensures that team members have a clear understanding of what they are trying to accomplish. Clarity of the goal can help reduce future conflicts related to necessary tasks, determine resources needed to accomplish the objectives, and define when the goal is accomplished. An essential condition in applying the prerequisite tree is an agreement of everyone on the team that the goal is vital and that its implementation will bring benefits to both the individuals and the organization. A clear statement of the goal and persuasive reasons why the goal is important should be established in this first step. In Theory of Constraints, the team's objective is referred to as the "ambitious target."

2. LIST OBSTACLES TO IMPLEMENTING THE GOAL.

Implementing Step 2 involves asking team members to identify all the potential obstacles to achieving the team's goal. The process continues until team members see no more obstacles. During this process, there is no criticism in terms of whether the obstacle is really an important issue or not. Only the person who suggested an obstacle has the right to withdraw it. This ground rule is designed to eliminate the possibility that another, more vocal team member might prevent an item from remaining on the list. Other well-known problem-solving techniques, such as brainstorming and Nominal Group Technique, use similar approaches.

In order to implement the authentic model of teamwork, it is absolutely necessary to identify individual concerns first. In other words, we need to identify what each member sees as potential obstacles from his or her individual perspective. Keeping in mind that Generation Xers are highly individualistic, it is even more important to understand their needs and concerns before addressing how the goal of the team is to be accomplished. However, team members also need to understand that raising obstacles is not merely giving excuses for why the objective cannot be accomplished. Identifying obstacles requires finding ways to convert obstacles into clear action plans.

Obstacles coming from this process can be divided into three subgroups.

- *Obstacles related to implementation issues.* These may include training, resources, and procedures that the organization currently does not have in place and that are needed to successfully achieve the ambitious target.

- *Existing elements that need to be removed to accomplish the goal.* These might include policies, measurements, and behaviors that currently exist that block the implementation of the goal. For example, policies could be creating misalignments between authority and responsibility, or measurements could be promoting unhealthy competition among employees.

- *Obstacles related to personal issues,* such as time constraints, personal schedules, etc. Even though these personal obstacles may not be directly related to the ambitious target, they still need to be considered if they have the potential to prevent the team from achieving its goal.

3. DETERMINE INTERMEDIATE OBJECTIVES TO OVERCOME OBSTACLES.

Once the list of obstacles has been determined, solutions are given for each one. The specific solutions for each obstacle are referred to as "intermediate objectives." Intermediate objectives respond to individual needs of the team members. Each intermediate objective should be determined in such a way that either the obstacle disappears or its influence ceases to block achievement of the goal. For example, if an obstacle is stated as "We do not have the expertise to perform this task in this department," then possible intermediate objectives include (1) conducting a training program or (2) simplifying the task so additional expertise is not needed. In the first intermediate objective, providing training that brings required expertise to the department eliminates the obstacle. The second intermediate objective does not eliminate the obstacle, but it does create a situation in which the obstacle is irrelevant.

This procedure consists of taking an obstacle and then asking for suggestions as to how to overcome it. Preferably, the same person who raised the obstacle should be the one suggesting an intermediate objective to overcome it. This person may have a better understanding of the obstacle and, in many cases, may have already thought about potential actions to eliminate it. However, any other member of the team is also welcome to suggest alternative actions. Several intermediate objectives may be combined to overcome an obstacle, although, logically, the intermediate objective that is easiest to implement or the least expensive should be selected. If necessary, the team may have to do additional research to make a better decision in selecting the appropriate intermediate objective. The aim is to match each obstacle with the best corresponding intermediate objective that will overcome it.

It is also possible that a team will be unable to come up with a specific way to overcome an obstacle. In this case, it is recommended that the intermediate objective simply be written as the opposite of the obstacle. Then, at some point later in the process, a separate prerequisite tree can be performed on that intermediate objective. If separate analyses are conducted for difficult intermediate objectives, the team will have a set of interconnected prerequisite trees. Intermediate objectives are usually written in the present tense, as opposed to future tense, to help the team visualize the future. When writing objectives in present tense, the team will tend to focus more on the final result or outcome instead of on the process needed to accomplish the objective. After all, given a specific outcome, there are multiple ways to achieve it.

Completing Step 3 results in a final list of obstacles and intermediate objectives called the Intermediate Objective Table.

4. MAP THE IMPLEMENTATION SEQUENCE OF THE INTERMEDIATE OBJECTIVES.
At this point, the team should have a list of intermediate objectives that, if accomplished, will eliminate all obstacles in the way of achieving the team's goal. However, the intermediate objectives are likely to be a disorganized array of seemingly unrelated tasks. Step 4's task is to convert

this list into a linked plan. To accomplish this, intermediate objectives must be put into a logical sequence by determining which intermediate objective should be worked on first, second, and so on—and also which intermediate objectives can be worked on in parallel with other intermediate objectives.

To do this, team members need to figure out which intermediate objectives are direct, logical prerequisites for achieving the ambitious target. In other words, it is necessary to determine which intermediate objectives the team must have in place before it can claim that the ambitious target has been accomplished. These intermediate objectives may also have immediate prerequisites that are found using the same logic. The process continues until all intermediate objectives are connected either to the ambitious target or to another intermediate objective. The connection among them can be depicted using the prerequisite tree. The prerequisite tree represents the final plan in graphic form, including all intermediate objectives and the logical implementation sequence. Examples of prerequisite trees will be shown in the two case studies at the end of this chapter.

5. ASSIGN INTERMEDIATE OBJECTIVES TO TEAM MEMBERS.
Step 5 is to assign each intermediate objective to a pecific member of the team, with the objective of establishing responsibility and accountability for executing each intermediate objective. An intermediate objective may be the sole responsibility of an individual, but also may be assigned to a subteam. At the end, however, each intermediate objective should be owned by a specific person. An intermediate objective may also be assigned to two different people who will work on it separately, with the idea that later they will compare what they find. Nonetheless, to increase the likelihood of completion, one person should be responsible for each objective.

In addition to assigning objectives, a clear statement of the resources needed to accomplish the intermediate objectives must be prepared. Knowing the specific need for resources helps team members manage potential resource contention among team members and across other teams. It also aids in the estimation of the project costs, which may be necessary in order to calculate the expected return on investment.

An additional piece of information important for the successful achievement of the team's goal is an estimation of the duration of each intermediate objective. Team members and management need to have an idea of the duration of the project and the requirements for resources at every step of the implementation process. Finally, a clear statement of the expected outcome of each intermediate objective, which indicates that a task has reached completion, facilitates the transition of a task from one team member to another.

6. EXECUTE IMPLEMENTATION PLAN.

The prerequisite tree is a living document and undoubtedly will have flaws and omissions. However, if done properly, it is a reasonable estimation of how the implementation process will be executed. As the plan is running, new obstacles may be added to the list and others may be removed. Periodic review of the prerequisite tree is therefore useful throughout the process. Evaluation of the plan and its implementation will provide adequate feedback to avoid future pitfalls.

To facilitate control and communication during the implementation process, there are different project management programs available. This is even more relevant when the team project is too complex to handle manually and, hence, some type of computerized solution is needed. Remember that Generation Xers tend to be technically sophisticated, and they may encounter little discomfort in using groupware technology.

Two Case Studies

The first case study involves a company that was reporting excess inventory. An intergenerational team that used the prerequisite tree was put together to try to solve the inventory problem. The team was successful in accomplishing its ambitious target.

The second case study narrates the process a team of teachers went through to improve the troublesome environment in their school. With the help of a consultant, the team followed the prerequisite tree process to develop a plan. The school environment improved dramatically after one year.

Although these two cases are based on real situations, some of the information has been disguised to protect personal anonymity.

Application of a Prerequisite Tree to Develop Team Consensus in a Distribution Company

THE TEAM AND THE FINAL OBJECTIVE

XYZ Parts Division provides replacement parts to customers worldwide. Over the years, XYZ's inventory has accumulated excess parts. Although some of these parts are still active, the amount in stock far exceeds any reasonable future demand. In addition, XYZ's current customers no longer need many of these parts, which are therefore classified as obsolete. The number of excess parts, inactive parts, and obsolete parts continues to grow, and XYZ's management wants to limit or reduce the size of inventory. Currently, XYZ's revenues are not meeting expectations and are not growing at the desired rate. Many customers are taking their business elsewhere because the parts they want to purchase are not readily available in XYZ's inventory, which further decreases revenue. More pressure builds to add new parts and to beef up stocking levels of other parts. A conflict exists between the desire to limit the cost of inventory and a desire to increase the availability to customers of needed inventory.

A cross-functional project team was assembled to determine a course of action. The team consisted of representatives from all pertinent domains of the company. The makeup of the team spanned a wide range of experience and a significant age spectrum. As would be expected, there were important issues of consensus building that had to be addressed if a cohesive plan was to be constructed by this team. Table 1 briefly identifies the domains, ages, and experience levels of the members of this team.

BUILDING A CONSENSUS PLAN UTILIZING A PREREQUISITE TREE

The team had several objectives. Implementation plans were developed for each objective, but, for the purposes of this case study, we show the results of only one of these objectives.

The objective was to reduce slow-moving, surplus, and obsolete inventory. The team had agreed that if this objective could be achieved, the

TABLE 1 *Team Members*

NAME	AGE	DOMAIN	PARTICIPATION	PLANNING EXPERIENCE
Jerry	51	Facilitator	Full Time	10
Tom	40	Process Improvement	Full Time	7
Risa	32	Purchasing	Full Time	2
Dan	34	Receiving	Full Time	1
Trini	25	Inventory Control	Full Time	1
Robbi	23	Shipping	Full Time	1
Tim	36	Operational Systems	Full Time	6
Kevin	31	Kitting and Projects	Full Time	3
Todd	37	Operational Management	Full Time	5
Perry	52	Information Systems	Full Time	7
Beau	29	Inventory Management	Full Time	3
Chip	35	Sales and Marketing	Part Time	2
Felecia	39	Finance and Accounting	Part Time	5
Brett	24	Customer Service	Part Time	1
Mark	40	Executive Sponsor	Part Time	7

pressing business problems would be well addressed. Everyone could see several roadblocks and pitfalls that precluded a smooth working environment. Building a prerequisite tree helped the team achieve its ambitious target.

The first step in bringing order out of the chaos was to allow everyone, in turn, to identify obstacles so that each could be addressed. A list of obstacles was thus constructed, and the obstacles were logically organized into associated groups. Then the task of sequencing the obstacles was addressed: which obstacles had to be overcome first, second, third, and so on. At this point, a prerequisite tree could be constructed. The bottom of the tree listed the first obstacle to be addressed and the associated intermediate objective that would overcome the obstacle. Then, obstacle by obstacle, each additional intermediate objective was added to the tree.

The main advantage of the tree approach is its stepwise refinement of the problem analysis and the focusing of effort that it facilitates. Both

TABLE 2 *Intermediate Objective Table for XYZ Parts Division*

Objective: To reduce slow-moving, surplus, and obsolete inventory

Obstacles	Intermediate Objectives
The demand for many parts that XYZ distributes is understated due to the lack of data being captured at time of order entry with regard to "fill or kill" orders.	A program of improved data capture is implemented.
Current poor communication between entities inside and outside XYZ creates many planning and forecasting disconnects.	Improved coordination and communication is established and embraced by all related entities.
We currently have no formal plan or methodology for processing returns from customers so that they do not adversely affect the quality of our inventory.	A formal plan and methodology for processing returns from customers so that they do not adversely affect the quality of our inventory is implemented.
We currently do not have a plan for the disposition of slow-moving, surplus, and obsolete parts.	A plan for the disposition of slow-moving, surplus, and obsolete parts is implemented.
Many customers and suppliers do not have confidence in our forecasting or other programs because we have not been able to deliver as expected in the past. This detracts from our ability to convince our suppliers to participate in new initiatives.	Customer and supplier buy-in to the Apollo project as envisioned is obtained.
Suppliers are currently complaining that they are overloaded with information regarding the multiple XYZ programs and initiatives.	All initiatives are coordinated and consolidated into the Apollo project.
We have many of the same suppliers doing business with multiple XYZ business entities in an uncoordinated manner with no single point of relationship management in existence.	A plan for coordinating multi-entity supplier relationships is created and implemented.
We currently do not have a detailed list of potential supplier coordination conflicts.	A detailed list of potential supplier coordination conflicts is developed.

Obstacles	Intermediate Objectives
Many of our current suppliers are not operationally ready to meet the demands of our business requirements.	A detailed supplier readiness and participation plan exists, and minimum supplier performance requirements are established.
We do not currently know the readiness level of our suppliers to be able to accommodate requirements we have for improving our supply chain performance.	A supplier readiness assessment is conducted and supplier readiness is known.
Relationships with many of our suppliers are informal and not well defined as to performance expectations.	A program of formal supplier relationship management is established and performance expectations are clearly identified, communicated, and accepted by all parties.
Supply chain management methodologies do not currently exist formally in XYZ operations.	XYZ identifies and adopts a program of formal supply chain management methodologies.

the experienced and less experienced members of the team became very comfortable with the process. Interactive tree building promotes excellent engagement from everyone. Regardless of their age or experience, participants had a strong sense that they were being heard and were equal contributors to the total solution. The result was team consensus. The constructed intermediate objective table and prerequisite tree are presented in table 2 and figure 4, respectively.

Many of the intermediate objectives are simply formed as the opposite of the obstacle. For example, "A plan for the disposition of slow-moving, surplus, and obsolete parts is implemented" is the opposite of "We currently do not have a plan for the disposition of slow-moving, surplus, and obsolete parts." This happens when a team's ambitious target is very general. Too many details will create a complicated plan with too many intermediate objectives. To continue the process, subteams may be assigned to specific intermediate objectives so that specific actions can be developed. Each subteam can apply the prerequisite tree process until a comfortable level of detail is found.

FIGURE 4 *Prerequisite Tree for XYZ Parts Division*

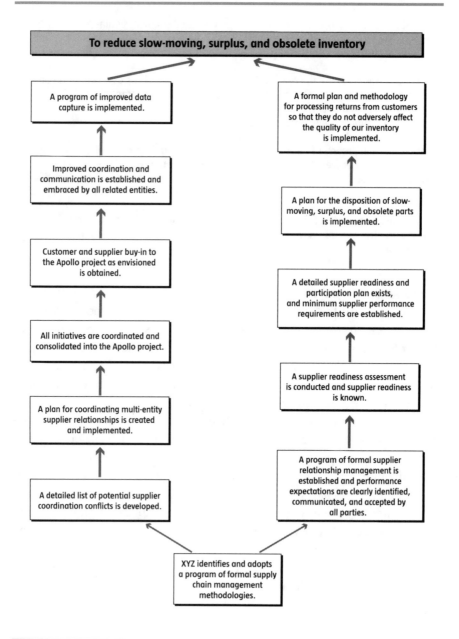

Application of a Tree to Improve the Environment of a Public School

This case study examines the application of the prerequisite tree in a school where the relationships among teachers and staff had become conflicted. The school staff was so divided that members were willing to do really bad things to each other. When using the phrase "bad things," we do not mean staff not speaking to each other or engaging in verbal abuse. We are talking about damaging cars, vandalizing rooms, reporting to the media, coercing parents to take sides, and making anonymous tattletale calls to the central administration office. The staff was divided on one strong issue, and, in the mind of each person you were either with them or against them. Any action by any person was viewed as an act of sabotage to the other side.

The school team was formed by first- and second-year teachers (mostly Generation Xers), experienced teachers (more than ten years of experience and Baby Boomers), and teachers who were ready to retire. The principal was a relatively young Baby Boomer.

Consultants brought in to help with the situation had experience working with teams that were in conflict, but, intuitively, they knew that this situation was far beyond the point where tried-and-true methodologies would work. They needed something that would remove blame and focus the staff on the issues, not each other.

The consultant used the prerequisite tree to guide the staff members in achieving the ambitious target of settling their differences and working together to achieve a common goal. The session started with a discussion leading toward the staff acknowledging its problems and accepting that they were everyone's problems. It was not difficult to get consensus on the current reality, "We continue to be a divided staff." In an attempt to move them toward developing an ambitious target, the consultant asked, "What would reality look like if this were not true?" "We would be a cohesive team" was the response. Eventually they settled on "We become a cohesive, high-performing team" as their ambitious target. Note that it was extremely important to dedicate time to achieving consensus on the ambitious target. Consensus is an important initial condition for the success of applying the prerequisite tree process.

TABLE 3 *Intermediate Objective Table for School's Conflicts*

Obstacles	Intermediate Objectives
There is a lack of communication among staff.	We communicate honestly and effectively.
There is back-stabbing going on.	We communicate honestly and effectively.
Rumors run rampant.	We communicate honestly and effectively.
Some are trying to sabotage others, pressuring them when they're not involved.	We communicate honestly and effectively.
Dishonesty is the norm.	We communicate honestly and effectively.
We have hurt and pain.	We acknowledge others'/our hurt and pain.
There is unwillingness to make changes.	We are willing to make a positive change.
We have lost friendships and relationships.	We choose to begin the healing process.
There is an inability to accept responsibility to apologize.	We choose to begin the healing process.
There is inappropriate communication going on with parents, media, and the central office.	We engage only in appropriate parental communications.
We choose not to understand the perspective of others.	We accept that others have different points of view.
We have little respect for the opinions of others.	We accept that others have different points of view.
We pressure others to become involved.	We accept that others have different points of view.
There are interruptions when someone wants to make a point.	We respect all members of our team.
There are too many (controlling) bosses.	We accept final authority.
Issues become personal confrontations.	We deal with the issues and not the people.

Obstacles	Intermediate Objectives
There is inconsistent protocol.	We follow protocol consistently.
There is lack of trust among staff.	Team members have more confidence in each other and others in the organization.
There is inconsistent support from the central office.	We have consistent, total support from the central office.
Good ideas are not accepted.	We are supportive of the positive achievements and ideas of our team.
There is jealousy among staff.	We are supportive of the positive achievements and ideas of our team.
We have bad publicity.	We have positive press.
Cliques, groups, and divisions exist.	We operate as a team.
There are feelings of alienation and isolation.	All staff members are part of the team.

The team spent an entire day uncovering every obstacle that was preventing achievement of this ambitious target. Table 3 shows the obstacles the staff uncovered. The situation was evidently critical, as some of the obstacles expressed included "There is back-stabbing going on" and "Issues become personal confrontations." Participants were then guided toward seeing reality as it could be if they did not have these specific obstacles blocking them. The team created intermediate objectives for the obstacles (see table 3). An important highlight from this process is the intermediate objective "We communicate honestly and effectively," which was enough to overcome several obstacles. This told the team how important this specific objective was for achieving the ambitious target. Of course, creating intermediate objectives also has the advantage of addressing all individual concerns raised in the previous step.

After creating the intermediate objectives, the staff sequenced them according to what must be accomplished first. The team chose "We are willing to make a positive change" and "We acknowledge others'/our hurt and pain" as the first two intermediate objectives to accomplish. The team needed to be prepared to change and to seek to understand others before any major change could be pursued. After these two intermediate objectives were accomplished, they would try to tackle the communication issues. The team followed a similar procedure and reasoning until the prerequisite tree was completed. The final prerequisite tree is shown in figure 5.

Because most intermediate objectives are somewhat general, specific actions were developed. Over the course of a year, tasks to accomplish these action steps were undertaken. For the intermediate objective "We communicate honestly and effectively," for example, some of the following actions were defined:

Control rumors by refusing to listen to rumormongers and not repeating unconfirmed information.

Identify people who feed on spreading rumors and do not share information with them.

Get to know each other to build trust by serving on committees to work on our problems, participating in Friday breakfast, and encouraging social committee to plan affairs for the staff.

When I misstep, be forgiving.

Read communications from principal.

Continue publishing the school newspaper.

These more specific steps support the intermediate objective. The same exercise was executed for all intermediate objectives, and nearly seventy actions were defined from the analysis.

To keep the momentum going, monthly workshops were conducted to encourage and guide the staff toward achieving its ambitious target. As a result of the team effort, the entire school year was free of overt clashes between staff members. This was indeed an incredible achievement considering that previous consultants, using traditional approaches, were sabotaged and literally run out of the school by the staff. The

FIGURE 5 *Prerequisite Tree for School's Conflict*

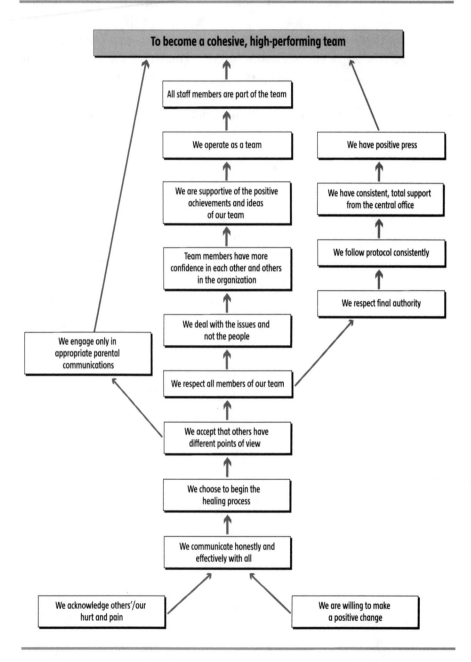

principal credits the Theory of Constraints process used in the two-day workshop just before school started for the smooth opening of school. (Our thanks to Cheryl Edwards for contributing to this case.)

These two studies illustrate the prerequisite tree process in practice as an application of the authentic model. The first case was primarily task-oriented, and the second case was process-oriented. However, the same logical principles apply: Ensure that individual concerns are addressed first before a link to the team's objective is established.

CHAPTER 6

Working with the Adversary Relationship

Almost all organizations today are composed primarily of people from both Generation X and the Baby Boom generation. A few high-tech, "dot com" systems are composed almost solely of Xers, and some entrenched government bureaucracies are made up almost exclusively of Boomers. There are some organizations that experience no problems between the generations, and there are a few that are practically deadlocked because of the unwillingness of both generations to work together. In short, there is a tremendously wide range in which this problem exists.

The research discussed in chapter 1 has shown that there are some very real and unexpected differences in values between the generations. Further, the literature has demonstrated that friction between Boomers and Xers is generally pervasive. We therefore have a potential for conflict. Conflict per se is all right, but when it occurs in a state of no tolerance, we have the beginnings of an adversarial relationship.

In looking at developing positive team attitudes and behaviors, collaboration is the long-term objective. Collaboration is the process by which synergy is created. Synergy is what most differentiates a team from a group. Synergy is to teams what energy is to an individual. It is defined here as "the whole being greater than the sum of its parts." Team members working together actually create energy. The combined amount of energy produced by the team is greater than the sum of the individual energies of its members.

Collaboration implies mutual strong commitment to the team objective, a willingness to confront ideas openly, an ability to manage conflict effectively, and a commitment to consensus as the preferred decision-making process. Collaboration can be easy or difficult to reach, depending on the working relationships among the team members and how authentic those relationships are.

The intermediate objective is cooperation. Cooperation implies a mutual recognition of the importance of the group objective. It demands a nonhostile relationship among team members and a willingness to listen to all positions. Conflict is frequently avoided. While consensus is desirable if attainable, majority rule is also an acceptable method for reaching decisions if all agree that their positions have been fairly considered.

The short-term, immediate goal is tolerance. Tolerance is the necessary first condition for creating more productive working relationships within a team. Tolerance implies that each group member of each generation has the right to hold personal views about the other generation but also has the responsibility to recognize that each member of the other generation has a right to be there and has something of value to contribute. Tolerance implies the necessity for co-existence and the willingness to allow others to express opposing views, openly and honestly: While I may choose not to tell you what I am thinking or feeling, what I do disclose, you can believe.

Most of the traditional work in team building has revolved around building consensus and developing a collaborative approach to conflict management. This is fine as long as all members of the team are ready to proceed to that level. This doesn't work when people pretend to be ready to collaborate because they want to be well thought of or feel that that is how they should be. Things go well on the surface until something divisive emerges. Then collaboration is avoided or abandoned altogether.

If organizations are going to evolve in new and more effective ways, emphasis should be placed on how things are, rather than how they should be. If tolerance is lacking in a group because of generational or other critical differences, these differences must be addressed first. Once tolerance is truly achieved, the group can begin its transformation into a team and the likelihood of its moving through cooperation into collaboration is greatly enhanced. If tolerance is never achieved, good work can still be accomplished. However, if a state of tolerance does not exist within the group, there is a high probability that the group is either in, or moving toward, a state of adversarial relationships.

The Myth of the Natural Adversary

The natural adversary concept presupposes that because you are who you are and I am who I am, we will be in perpetual conflict. There are two very costly outcomes to this condition. The first is that, once I see you as a natural adversary, my tendency is to avoid direct contact with you in favor of gleaning and wallowing in negative information and rumors about you. More energy is spent in avoiding each other than in finding ways to work together more productively.

The second costly outcome is the creation of a self-fulfilling prophecy. That is, if you and I expect to be in conflict simply because we belong to different generations, we will tend to behave toward each other in ways that make the conflict unavoidable. When the conflict does eventually occur, we have "proven" our theory, and it now becomes the norm. There is much written about "natural adversaries" such as cats and dogs, cobras and mongooses, and whales and giant squid. The natural adversary relationship holds some credence when applied to some animal species, but it turns into pure myth when applied to humans. That is, we take the natural adversary relationship from nature and tend to apply it to relationships such as the Serbs and Croats, the Montagues and Capulets, Management and Labor, or Boomers and Xers, in exactly the same manner.

Although we may perceive some adversary relationships as being natural, they are not. If any two people, or two groups, are adversaries, it is strictly by conscious choice. Seeing things differently, wanting different things, and even holding different values is natural and forms the source of energy and creativity.

The potential for real damage begins when an adversarial position begins to turn into an adversarial relationship. When this happens, stereotyping replaces awareness, and both sides begin to build "ogres." With each passing day, our cause and characteristics become more righteous and theirs more reprehensible. As time passes, the gap widens and the problem tends to increase. This phenomenon can be witnessed in individual relationships—for example, sisters who brag that they haven't spoken to each other in thirty-five years—right on up to national identities such as the Greeks and the Turks. Boomers and Xers are certainly not immune.

In breaking the adversary relationship, the immediate objective is not to have both groups start to get along well. Instead, the objective is to restructure and normalize the relationship so that conflict can be managed constructively. The initial position of tolerance can thus be regained. The long-term goal is to have all parties working collaboratively.

Distinguishing Characteristics of the Adversary Relationship

The adversary relationship is a unique form of nonproductive conflict and varies from other types of conflict in six different ways.

1. Other forms of nonproductive conflict are primarily concerned with misperceptions about issues. Adversary relationship conflict is primarily concerned with misperceptions about people.

   Nonproductive conflict: "I flatly disagree with their interpretation."
   Adversary relationship conflict: "These people are just too stupid to see what's happening."

2. Other forms of nonproductive conflict usually result from poor contact and communications among people. Adversary relationships are usually the result of no contact among people.

   Nonproductive conflict: "I just got off the phone with one of them, and I couldn't get a word in edgewise."
   Adversary relationship conflict: "There's no point in talking with these people. We know how they are going to react."

3. Other forms of acute nonproductive conflict are quite uncomfortable for the parties involved. Adversary relationships are chronic in nature and not only are uncomfortable but often provide the adversaries a reason for being, as in family feuds such as the Hatfields and the McCoys.

   Nonproductive conflict: "The thought of having to deal with them in the project meeting tomorrow makes my blood run cold."
   Adversary relationship conflict: "We've always known what they were like. Here they go again."

4. Other forms of nonproductive conflict occur in a state of interdependence. Both sides still need something from each other to gain a specific end. In adversary relationships, both groups tend to see each other as not now and not ever being of any use to each other or to the organization.

   Nonproductive conflict: "I hate to admit it, but without their engineering talent, we don't stand a chance of winning the contract."
   Adversary relationship conflict: "They never have, they don't now, and they never will have anything of value to contribute."

5. In other forms of nonproductive conflict, both adversaries can temporarily walk away from the conflict if the present situation is mutually dire or threatening enough. In adversary relationships, the feelings of hatred and/or contempt are so deeply rooted that enduring any outcome is preferable to letting go of the relationship. This frequently takes the form of "We don't care if we win or not, as long as they don't."

   Nonproductive conflict: "Did you see the VP's face during that last argument? We'd better cool it a little."
   Adversary relationship conflict: "They're evil and self-serving, and our obligation is to warn the organization. I don't care what the cost is."

6. The last distinction is the most destructive of all. In other forms of nonproductive conflict, the desired outcome is cast in terms of things that are wanted by both sides yet are under dispute. The worst that each side wishes is that they will win and the other side will lose. In the adversary relationship, the desired outcome is to injure or destroy the opponent if at all possible.

Nonproductive conflict: "Hooray! We won!"
Adversary relationship conflict: "Hooray! They lost!"

Adversary Relationships and Generation Conflict

Generation conflict has the potential to become adversarial. On the one hand, you have the Boomer whose basic view is, "Hell, it's not like when I was a boy! These kids just don't value work or company loyalty today." On the other hand, you have the Xer, whose initial reaction is, "These old geezers are doing it the same way they did thirty years ago. You can't teach them anything. Besides, I'm sick of listening to how they had to walk five miles to school and back barefoot in the snow every day, going uphill both ways." As the adversary relationship is cast in terms of generation identities rather than individual identities, the problem will be perpetuated.

As previously mentioned, not all relationships between the generations are necessarily conflicted, and, of those that are, not all are adversarial. Nevertheless, it is always much easier to avoid an adversary relationship between Xers and Boomers than it is to halt one.

Avoiding The Adversary Relationship

Several potential pitfalls of adversary relationships can be avoided by becoming aware of them.

First, don't breed competition between the groups. Competition is an appropriate conflict model when focused outside the organization, and it is the only appropriate conflict model in the field of athletics. Competition is based on win/lose, and everyone competing for his or her share of the market or the winning score understands this. As such, competition is totally inappropriate as a means of motivating workers to outperform their co-workers. Tactics such as sales contests breed much more internal destruction than they do productivity, particularly when the competitors are interdependent and somehow need each other to meet the objective. It is never wise to turn a destructive force inward. This suggests that care needs to be taken not to inadvertently play one group against the other, particularly when making comparisons.

Second, know what behavior you are rewarding. Over and above pay, promotion, recognition, bonuses, and other formalized means of rewarding behavior, much subtler forms of rewards and punishments occur in the work setting: Who gets the first offer of overtime? Who does the boss avoid at coffee breaks? Who is not asked for advice? All these are very subtle and very effective shapers of ongoing behavior. A few guidelines to keep in mind when considering ongoing rewards are

- *Be clear about what you want.* Do you want Xers and Boomers to get along with each other better, or do you want them to work better together? These are frequently not the same thing and have a lot to do with how you reward and punish conflict.

- *Be aware of what you are using for rewards.* Don't sell your time or personal impact short. Don't underestimate the value of a quick recognition for good work or the resentment that can arise from it being unexpressed.

- *Focus on equity, not equality.* It is impossible to give everyone equal amounts of everything, and very few people want it that way anyway. Xers and Boomers are driven by different types of external rewards. Use the Platinum Rule: "Do unto others as others would have done unto them."

- *Focus on rewards rather than punishment.* While sometimes discipline is appropriate, more will be gained by giving and withholding rewards. Boomers will be more tolerant, although no less hating, of punishments, whereas Xers will be much less tolerant.

- *Don't compare generation members to each other.* If an Xer screws up, deal with the mistake, but not by comparing his or her behavior to the more appropriate behavior of a typical Boomer. All this will do is exacerbate the problem. I can't recall a single case where being asked "Why can't you be more like your brother?" resulted in bringing the brothers closer together.

Third, avoid the adversary relationship by avoiding dehumanizing the adversary. Regardless of which generation you belong to, be careful about how you refer to the other, particularly when you are frustrated by one of them. Dehumanization is the act, intentional or not, of robbing people of their dignity and making them seem less than human in their own eyes. This is usually brought about by sarcasm, stereotyping, derision, disenfranchisement, removing options, and, by far the worst of all, nonresponsiveness. The implied message is "You don't exist."

Policies and rules instituted for the betterment of the organization and its members sometimes favor one group over another. Seniority will certainly have this effect if it is the principle on which reward or opportunity is based. If such is the case, make sure that Xers are also acknowledged and provided for.

Fourth, keeping the work meaningful helps avoid the adversary relationship. A raft of literature points to the fact that motivation is an internal process. People are motivated when they are doing something because they want to do it. By structuring work so that it becomes meaningful to a worker, more energy will be put into the work done by the worker. The less there is in a job to draw the interest and energy of the employee, the more time the worker has to reflect on perceived injuries, insults, and just how unacceptable the other group is becoming. Faced with meaningless work for an indefinite period, a bored worker can always scare up a hate campaign for lack of anything more creative to do.

Halting the Adversary Relationship

Although the suggestions above will help avoid situations wherein an adversary relationship can occur between Xers and Boomers, there are no easy steps to ensure a positive outcome if a relationship does in fact become adversarial. The following six-step process, however, can be used to stop the relationship from getting any worse. This process may also get both sides to develop some honest tolerance for each other.

STEP 1: BOTH GROUPS MUST DECIDE THAT THEY WANT TO CHANGE THE RELATIONSHIP.

The real irony in established adversary relationships is that the longer both sides are involved in being adversaries, the more deeply committed they become to keeping things the way they are. Unless both sides recognize that it is to their respective advantage to begin normalizing their working relationship, nothing of value will occur. It's like forcing two kids to shake hands before the fight is over.

Both sides can be coerced into pretending to work on the problem. They can also be let alone until they bring themselves, and the organization, to the brink of disaster. These solutions should obviously be avoided if at all possible. The peacemaker must try to get both sides to see that it is not to their advantage to maintain the status quo. This is usually brought about by a process known as "pain transfer."

Pain transfer does not imply that anyone should physically or psychologically hurt anyone else. It refers to the process of getting people to take full responsibility for their own actions and choices. In many adversary relationships, the adversaries take the moral high ground, a reason to be on the attack. Life is much more interesting simply because the adversary relationship exists. The person or persons who are "in pain" are those who have to put up with the ever-increasing tension that the relationship creates, the loss of productivity that occurs as a result of the adversaries refusing to work together, and the steadily diminishing group cohesion that this condition produces.

It certainly costs very little to begin the process by appealing to everyone's reason and better natures. Chances are, however, that this approach—sane as it is—will be ineffective in getting people to reprogram their relationships.

As a manager who must deal with this issue, the essential first step is to transfer the pain from you to the individuals who are adversaries. No reason exists for them to consider making a change—just because it would make life less stressful for you. Instead, make clear statements about what will occur if the condition continues to deteriorate, and let the adversaries know how that condition will directly affect their work lives. We are not suggestiong that you deliver threats or ultimatums, but, rather, that you provide a clear perspective about how things are going and what the eventual outcomes are likely to be. Focus on issues such as the loss of sales or market share, increased waste, declining morale, and upper management's increasing annoyance with the situation. Get the adversaries in touch with what it will cost them to continue the conflict.

STEP 2: CONSIDER USING A FACILITATOR.

Because in an adversary relationship neither side is particularly anxious to hear what the other side has to say, have a third party manage the process. The facilitator can be a management consultant, a human resources manager, or anyone who has the requisite skills. The individual chosen as facilitator should

- Be seen as a friend to both sides or be seen as neutral by both sides

- Have no personal investment in the outcome

- Have good interpersonal skills

- Have some experience, or at least no discomfort, working with conflict

- Have some commitment to a positive outcome, regardless of what it is

- Be reasonably patient

- Be skilled in "active listening"

Once both sides have agreed on a facilitator, a contract between the facilitator and the adversaries needs to be developed. This needs to be done before any work begins in modifying the relationship. The contract should include, but not be limited to, the following elements:

1. The facilitator will respect the confidentiality of anything that is said in private unless express permission to disclose is given by the speaker.

2. The facilitator has a right to refuse to act as a go-between for the adversaries. While the facilitator can occasionally choose to act in this capacity, it is best avoided. The adversaries are already not talking to each other, and acting as a messenger gives tacit approval to the present state of affairs.

3. The facilitator will not take sides. The facilitator's effectiveness depends on being seen as neutral and a supporter of the process.

Anything that brings the facilitator's neutrality into question has a probability of derailing the whole process.

4. The facilitator may state a personal opinion. This is quite different from taking sides. The facilitator is in the unique position of being part of a process but having no personal investment in any particular outcome. This provides a perspective that is unavailable to either side. So long as the facilitator takes ownership of the opinion or observation, it becomes just one more alternative to consider and can be quite valuable in that context.

5. The facilitator speaks the "unspeakable." There are many types of statements that are unsafe for adversaries to make to each other in such a volatile situation. Over and above generational issues, there may be personal enmities, differences in organizational rank, or unfinished business between the adversaries that is retarding the process. These "hidden agendas" may be very obvious to all concerned, but so long as they remain unstated, they are a block to progress. The facilitator may be the only one who feels safe to say, "What I think is not being said here is . . . ," and then check to see if it is an issue.

Once the facilitator has presented the "contract" for approval, ask the adversaries if there is anything that they would like added that would support a safer, more open environment.

Once established in the role, the facilitator has two functions to perform. The first is to keep communications open between the two adversaries, and the second is to manage the conflict between them as it occurs. Both these functions are accomplished through active listening, or paraphrasing what is being said; airing hidden agendas; making sure that each person is speaking strictly for her- or himself; keeping people to the point; making sure that any agreements made are time-bounded and clearly understood by both sides; and maintaining the dignity of all people who are party to the process.

STEP 3: CLARIFY POSITIONS.

The instinctive approach when dealing with adversary relationships is to get both parties to see the error of their ways. While this seems to make sense, the usual outcome of trying to get people to see that they have been wrong is that they justify their past positions and then continue to resist any move to get them to change. An alternative approach has a better probability of working.

If you have been effective in transferring the pain, two conditions exist. First is the intensity of the adversary relationship, and second is the awareness that something has changed in the environment that says it's now appropriate to explore the possibility of working toward a solution. Both elements must be honored: the current state of the relationship and the change in circumstances.

Once it is established that both adversaries have a right to different views, have each side present its position as clearly as the situation allows. Note that if the relationship has a high potential for volatility, each side should be encouraged to disclose only as much as it feels safe in stating. Sometimes it takes time to build the requisite trust for full disclosure, and the process shouldn't be rushed.

An example of how this process works is drawn from some early work done with interracial relationships in several large organizations. The purpose of the programs was to work on discrimination; however, by mutual consent, the groups chose rather to work with prejudice.

First, the group established the norm that for the duration of the program, it was okay to be prejudiced and to own up to it. The assumption was that prejudice probably existed to some degree on both sides and that both parties needed to recognize and legitimize what was occurring now.

Then the total group was asked to break up into two subgroups, one white and the other black. Some whites felt more aligned with the black group and joined them.

Next, each group was asked to generate two lists of adjectives. The first list was in response to the question "What are they like?" The second list was in response to the question "What will they say we are like?"

The first group was asked to expose its responses to "What will they say we are like?" and the second group disclosed its list of responses to "What are they like?" A comparison was made between the lists, and the process was then repeated for the second group.

In all cases, both groups' responses to "What are they like?" were more positive and better balanced than were their responses to "What will they say we are like?" That is, both groups had a more balanced and fairer view of the other group than the other group guessed they would have.

Whether the groups are divided according to race or according to generation, most of a group's assumptions about any other group are founded in prejudice and/or stereotyping. No one has to justify or explain why he or she feels the way he or she does, only how or what he or she feels. This process provides an awareness based on current perception, rather than myth-based assumptions, and is the beginning of creating a dialogue.

In presenting initial perceptions and positions, when one adversary states her initial impression to the other adversary, she can't tell him how he is, and he can't tell her what she sees or feels. The whole purpose of this exercise is to have each side aware of how it is seen by the other so that it can begin to make corrections in the other group's misperceptions.

STEP 4: REDEFINE ROLES IN THE LIGHT OF CURRENT CONDITIONS.

Once the adversaries have agreed that they may both benefit from reevaluating the relationship (Step 1), have decided if they wish to use a facilitator (Step 2), and are relatively comfortable with their own position and somewhat tolerant of the other's (Step 3), the next step is to redefine the roles in terms of what is going on right now.

Sometimes external pressures are so great that little choice exists but for both sides to bury their differences and temporarily cooperate. The problem is that once the external pressure for change is reduced or gone, the old animosities and myths tend to reappear, particularly if nothing has been done to address them. Probably the best example of this was seen in the war of the Balkans. Yugoslavia enjoyed relative internal harmony under Tito's rule until the Communist state fell. Once the pressure to conform was gone, the ancient prejudices and hatreds returned with a vengeance. This phenomenon can occur to a lesser extent in any long-term adversary relationship because so much energy has been invested in maintaining the adversarial positions for so long.

When initial positions have been stated and understood and when mutual awareness exists that a less hostile stance might be to everyone's advantage, look for potential common ground. The best way to redefine roles is in terms of present wants and concerns.

Wants At this point, distrust has been reduced to a workable level. Both sides now disengage and develop two lists. The first list is "What do we want for the team?" and the second list is "What would I like for myself?" Both lists are important. While there is a wide range of response, the expectation is that Boomers will be more focused on what is wanted for the group. Xers will probably be more focused on "What's in it for me?" An important benefit of this is that both groups recognize the legitimacy of both perspectives.

A second benefit for generating the "What would I like for myself?" list is that if a state of mistrust has existed for a long time, I am not going to trust your perceptions about wanting what's best for the group (me) very much. However, if I can see what's in it for you in cooperating with me, I can trust your input more. Putting a value on enlightened self-interest is one way of getting the relationship re-aligned more realistically.

When each group begins to develop its lists, several criteria need to be operative. First, no justification for a want is ever necessary. People are going to want whatever it is they want, no matter who says they should or shouldn't. It's enough that they are clear about what is desired and are willing to state it openly.

Second, the want must be specific and outcome-oriented, rather than a request that people attempt to change who they are. For example, "I'd like Pete to respond to my e-mail within the hour when possible" is far more attainable than "I want Pete to be more communicative."

Third, the want must be time-bounded whenever possible. By including when the want is to be achieved, it is more likely that a priority will be placed on it. Anything that isn't time-bounded, regardless of its real importance, tends to end up in the "first chance I get" bin.

Concerns When roles are being redefined, address what is not wanted by both parties as well. Because each new situation holds potential for negative as well as positive outcomes, ask the parties to be clear on what new concerns they have about what might occur as things progress.

Known risks can arise when adversaries state their concerns to each other. The most obvious risk occurs when one side states its concerns, and the other side now knows where it is vulnerable and can take advantage of that. There is also risk, though, if either side does not state concerns openly; then they are back to keeping it bottled up and having it turn into myth and negative stereotype. At that point, they incur a greater risk of the other side inadvertently hurting them because the adversary does not know where their vulnerabilities lie.

Have adversaries state their concerns openly but cautiously. As with the "wants," the open stating of concerns is a necessary part of establishing a minimum level of trust between the adversaries. The trust level is essential to restructuring the relationship in a more positive and permanent way. Note that trust translates into the statement "I will do nothing to intentionally harm you."

STEP 5: DEVELOP A CONTRACT.

Just as it is essential that a contract be developed between the facilitator and the adversaries before any work begins, so it is necessary to negotiate a contract between the adversaries themselves. Creating a set of guidelines that will provide a relatively safe environment reduces defensiveness and oversensitivity toward the other group once the work has started. Paradoxically, working on the contract is usually the first successful cooperative endeavor that the adversaries accomplish together.

In the early stages of the work, you can almost bank on the fact that if there is any ambiguity in what is being said by one side, the worst possible interpretation will be placed on it by the other. The objective of the contract is to normalize working relationships among the adversaries, and the more mechanical the contract is, the higher the probability of this outcome occurring.

There are several advantages to taking the time to negotiate a contract when dealing with an adversary relationship. First, the contract clearly outlines what behaviors and actions will and will not be appropriate. This removes some points of vulnerability at the outset, such as, "No name-calling" or "Speak only for yourself." Second, it provides the adversaries with a clear, mutually agreed-on path for dealing with one another. Third, it provides a means of redress so that if a violation does occur, it can be dealt with specifically and the whole process won't be derailed. Fourth, the negotiation is a dry run of the entire process. That is, the parties have to come together and state their wants and concerns openly in order to negotiate the contract.

Negotiating the contract is the initial business that both sides conduct together. Usually the facilitator first explains the purpose of the contract and then presents the contract to the total group for "ratification." Both sides are encouraged to question and suggest modifications to any element presented, so that, when complete, all parties agree on what will constitute acceptable behavior throughout the process of exploring their differences.

The contract needs to be flexible and responsive to the particular situation and the individuals involved. Most contracts contain, at least, these five elements:

- Purpose of the meeting

- Definition of areas of individual responsibility

- Agreed-on guidelines for dealing with communications and conflict

- How demands will be made and answered

- Rules for disengagement

STEP 6: THE PROCESS

The facilitator will be the one who chooses what format the process will follow. This is done with the concurrence of both sides. There is no one best way to conduct these kinds of meetings; the two options presented below demonstrate the breadth of possibilities. Generally, the facilitator will develop a proposed format and then run it by each group, or the reresentatives of each group, prior to the actual meeting. This has the effect of getting a mutual buy-in to the process and also precludes the possibility of something being an unwelcome surprise to any of the group members.

If the relationship between Boomers and Xers has reached a truly adversarial condition, then the first part of any meeting has to deal with challenging the perceptions that each holds of the other. Again, the purpose is to develop a genuine minimal level of mutual tolerance and trust that will allow the energy to be shifted away from interpersonal issues and redirected toward performance issues. The following techniques are appropriate for working with both interpersonal issues and work-related concerns.

The Fish Bowl   The Fish Bowl is a meeting format that allows a lot of information to be shared in a nonthreatening manner. It is conducted in the following manner:

1. One group, for example, the Boomers, clusters in the center of the room, generally sitting in a circle on the floor.

2. The Xers sit on chairs encircling the Boomers.

3. The Boomers are directed to talk among themselves about the way they see things, concerns they have, their view of the Xers, and so forth. There is no time limit.

4. The Xers "eavesdrop." They are required to remain silent and listen, although provision can be made for them to ask for clarification, if needed. No comments may be made by them about what is being said.

5. When the Boomers are finished, they exchange places with the Xers and the process is repeated.

6. When finished, both groups disengage and discuss what they heard the other group say and how that influences their present views, perceptions, and wants.

7. The total group reconvenes and a representative from each side states what their current position is and what additional questions they might have for the other group.

Demand—Response   This process is much more formal and mechanistic than the Fish Bowl in that it provides more safety and clarity. The process begins with both groups working alone and developing a list of what they want from the other group. Each item on the list can be either something they want the other group to respond to or something they would like the other group to simply understand. When the list is complete, the groups come together and alternate in making demands on each other. The rules of engagement are as follows:

1. All demands must be introduced with the phrase "What I would like is . . . ."

2. All demands must be made to specific individuals.

3. All demands must be made in terms of specific behaviors or actions and include a target date. For example, "I would like Charlie to provide us with the project projections by the last day of this month." Or, "I would like Ann to say what's on her mind, rather than rolling her eyes and sighing, starting right now."

4. Any request for clarity of a demand must be phrased in terms of "what" or "how," never "why." Asking "why" somebody wants something forces the demander to justify his or her position. This is guaranteed to make things worse.

5. All responses to demands must be made using one of these three expressions: "Yes, I will," "No, I won't," or "Yes, I will under the following circumstances . . . ." This last choice represents a counteroffer, and the original demander can respond to this counteroffer with one of the three phrases above.

6. Things that one group wants the other to understand are simply stated and require no response from the other group, such as, "What I would like you to understand is that I have a hard time relating to long stories about how things were here twenty years ago."

Once a demand has been accepted, it's written down and an agreement is made.

Suppose that an Xer has agreed to meet the request of a Boomer. If something happens that prevents the Xer from meeting the obligation, the Xer informs the Boomer as soon as possible, and the target date is moved back or the situation is appropriately altered. If the Xer fails to meet the obligation by the agreed-on target date and fails to notify the Boomer in time, the Boomer is obligated to check out what happened with the Xer first, before drawing any conclusions or bringing it to others' attention.

Conclusions

As more and more Xers join the workforce and move into positions of increasing responsibility, more and more Boomers are staying on the job. Legislation has enabled Boomers to draw full Social Security benefits while staying employed full time. This points to the probability that these two generations will be working together much longer than either of them had anticipated. The first step toward creating a more tolerant atmo-sphere is for each generation to recognize just what it is that the other generation has to offer.

What the Boomers bring to the table: Experience, sense of group, long-term perspective, patience

What Xers bring to the table: Focus on the immediate, high-tech proficiency, balanced view, valuing the individual

Once true tolerance and minimal trust are established as a starting place, how can we develop managerial strategies and organizational structures that will support Generation X values while at the same time integrating both groups into effective teams?

Most of this book is dedicated to suggestions aimed at restructuring the environment to accommodate the needs and values of both generations and to begin to make room for the next generation. In the interim, groundwork can be established for effective interaction, if attention is devoted to managing the potential adversary relationships that can arise when different people have to work together to create a common outcome.

CHAPTER 7

Retaining Generation Xers

At a recent conference in Brussels dealing with recruiting and retention, one presenter began with a brief and telling anecdote. It seems
that a small but very effective high-tech company was in a state of
expansion. It had just hired a young Baby Boomer manager who had
good interpersonal skills. The executives thought he would be able to
effectively manage the Gen Xers who made up the largest part of the
workforce.

The first day on the job the Boomer manager called his staff together to lay out some ground rules. He informed the staff that he would
like them to remove all games from their computers, as this was inconsistent with the results orientation that the company was maintaining.
He did this in a very supportive and nonthreatening manner. One of the
Xers mumbled, "Whatever," and walked out of the room and out of the
organization. That Xer was working again for a new company in three
days. It took the company he left six months to find his replacement.

This brief anecdote highlights the fact that finding and keeping good
people is a growing problem that will continue for at least the next
decade. Two factors contribute to this situation. First, approximately

78 million Baby Boomers are in the workforce with approximately 45 million Gen Xers. Even with a lot of manufacturing going to offshore companies and technology automating a lot of what is left, not enough people exist to do the work as it is presently forecast. The problem here is one of recruitment.

Second, many Boomer-managed companies do not know how to retain the Xers that they do have and want to keep. Current research indicates that what it takes to retain an Xer is, in many cases, quite different from what it takes to retain a Boomer.

The Problem

In the United States over the past two decades, work has become significantly more information-intensive than labor-intensive. Technology has replaced muscle. One side effect is that when people do have to be replaced, the cost can become astronomic. For example, a recent article (Bliss 1999) stated that when considering all related costs, such as loss of productivity due to vacancy, recruiting, selection, training the new hire, customer dissatisfaction, and so forth, the total cost of replacing an employee is 150 percent of that person's annual salary and benefits package. Within sales and management positions, the replacement costs can run as high as 200 to 250 percent of the total compensation package for the position that has been vacated. One only has to look at the organization's payroll and multiply it by 150 percent (or more) to get some idea of how important retention has become in terms of the system's ability to survive and prosper.

Attracting and retaining the best people, however, is no longer just a matter of the compensation package or the nature of the position. It also involves understanding the population from which you are recruiting. Key differences, some of which have been discussed earlier, that bear most heavily on the issue of retention are

Boomers:	Work hard out of a sense of loyalty
Xers:	Work hard if there is a balance allowed between work and personal life

Boomers: Expect long-term employment
Xers: Expect to be fired or laid off at least once
(They saw it happen to their parents.)

Boomers: Rely on the organization
Xers: Rely on self

Boomers: Believe everyone starts at the bottom and pays his or her dues
Xers: Believe everybody is placed where most needed; dues aren't relevant

Boomers: Hold the long view; their most valued benefit is a good pension plan
Xers: Hold the short view; their most valued benefit is good working conditions

Boomers: Identify with the NFL: anonymous contribution with everyone knowing his part; the team is everything
Xers: Identify with the NBA: teamwork is essential but must support individual talent and effort

Boomers: Believe in waiting one's turn
Xers: Believe in seizing each and every opportunity as it arises

Boomers: Believe self-sacrifice is a virtue
Xers: Believe self-sacrifice might occasionally have to be endured

Boomers: High community orientation; belong to groups, which provide most of the social interaction
Xers: Low community orientation; friends made on the job and work teams provide community

Boomers: Experience "burnout"
Xers: Experience underutilization; need to feel appreciated

Boomers: Respect organizational status and authority
Xers: Question practices and values

Boomers: Tend to punish mistakes
Xers Tend to reward successes

Boomers: Politically active
Xers: Politically much less active (Less than 33 percent of this age group voted in the 1992 election as compared to 42 percent who voted in the 1972 election.)

Boomers: Believe in the Golden Rule: "Do unto others as you would have others do unto you"
Xers: Believe in the Platinum Rule: "Do unto others as others would have done unto them"

While not exhaustive, this comparison does indicate that we are definitely dealing with two "different breeds of cat." We have to start responding to these differences.

Critical Retention Factors

In looking at salient factors most critical to retaining Generation X employees, six categories emerge from the literature. These are

- Work environment

- Work content

- Growth opportunities

- Compensation and rewards

- Organizational culture

- Working relationships with managers and with co-workers

Although the elements that will retain Xers may also be effective in retaining Baby Boomers, Xers are less tolerant of the absence of these factors, such as challenging work, than Boomers. The following applications are suggested from the research and from other sources consistent with the implications of the research. You may discover in trying these applications that you have found a way to keep your best people from both generations a little longer.

Retention Factor 1: Work Environment

Gen Xers are much less impressed with formality and are significantly more individualistic, as determined by the research, than their older counterparts. Not to acknowledge their need for individual expression is to send a subtle message that "You really don't exist outside the identity of your group." No one will tolerate that message for long, regardless of generation identity. Factors in the environment that will have particular appeal to Gen X workers include the following.

PERMIT CASUAL ATTIRE.

Yablonka (1999) points out the need for casual attire. In our opinion, if you must have a day when people have to dress a certain way, make it "Dress Up Monday," rather than "Dress Down Friday." Better yet, get rid of the formal dress requirement altogether. We are not suggesting that you abandon the values and cultures of your organization, only that you scrutinize them in light of current realities and the need for worker retention. We are not advocating tastelessness, only informality.

To set new, more relaxed standards for dress not only shows responsiveness to younger employees, it reduces status differences and encourages more open communications among people who have to work together. A $1,500 three-piece suit has a much greater chance of drawing a snicker than a salute in today's work environment.

PROVIDE OFFICES RATHER THAN CUBICLES.

Individuality is critical to the Xers and so is the opportunity to express it. Office cubicles, a more efficient and cost-effective use of space, are also heavily counter-cultural for most Xers (Merrick 1998). Cubicles give the illusion, but not the reality, of privacy.

Recognizing that reconfiguring office space is a tremendously expensive endeavor (look what it cost you to create the cubicle warren), you might want to have human resources do an attitude survey just to make sure that it isn't creating a level of dissatisfaction that you really can't afford. That is, it might cost you more in potential turnover to leave it as is than to change it.

ALLOW FOR PERSONALIZATION OF WORKSPACE.

Regardless of how the workspace is configured, the more you encourage the personalizing of it, the better off everyone will be. One very telling example of this was reported on ABC's *Nightline* (Smith 1999). An employee of an extremely successful product design company requested that the company buy a wing off a DC-3 airplane (for $4,000) simply to decorate the work area. The request was granted. When questioned as to why the company was willing to spend this money, the boss said, "That's decor. That's ambience. You know, that says we're weird and we're proud of it."

The real question here is, did the company provide the wing because it was successful, or was the company successful because it provided the wing? There's little question that the company clearly sees it as the latter case. The point is that the more you encourage individuality and the expression of it, the higher the probability that you will be able to keep the people who are providing results for you.

Retention Factor 2: Work Content

This factor more than any other is equally essential for retaining both Baby Boomers and Gen Xers. Woker states, "The industry must realize that the era of long-term job security has been replaced by the need for interesting work and opportunity among the present crop of workers" (1999, p. 60). Members of both generations will quit when stuck with chronically dull, meaningless, repetitive work. The only real difference lies in how the respective generations express "quitting." Gen Xers will leave you for competitors who will provide work that is more fun, challenging, and exciting. Baby Boomers will stay on, drawing a paycheck and doing the bare minimum, until they can retire.

Work content addresses the capacity of the work to provide motivation to the employee. The rather archaic view that money motivates is still held dear by many executive Baby Boomers. There is no question that people have to work to make a living. Money is critically important in keeping them from wandering off until it is time to go home. Yet, money has absolutely nothing to do with the quality of work or the energy that is put into it. These factors are almost solely controlled by the nature of the work itself.

An interesting confirmation of this perspective (Merrick 1998) was presented in the 1998 Career and Salary Survey, which reported that salary and compensation was ranked sixth in "Most Satisfying Aspects of the Job." It followed, in rank order, "Solving challenging problems," "People you work with," "Interesting work/variety of work," "Doing what you're good at," and "Ability to work independently."

MAKE THE WORK FUN.

Common wisdom used to be that medicine had to taste bad and work had to be solemn business. Fortunately, both myths have been exploded. On average, adults spend more waking hours at work than at any other single place, including their homes. Maintaining the quality of life is as important a factor on the job as it is in the home environment, and simply "having a good time" is an essential part of that.

Probably the most valuable resource an organization has to meet its objectives is worker energy. Fun creates "energy" on the job, whether that comes from being absorbed in a challenging problem, working collaboratively with close colleagues, or simply having a good laugh. Energy keeps people engaged. Taking a short break from a puzzling problem by playing a few quick games of solitaire can be much more productive than staring at a blank screen as the frustration continues to deepen.

FOSTER FREEDOM OF DECISION MAKING.

A raft of literature strongly points to the fact that people, regardless of age grouping, respond better and are more committed when they are dealt with as contributors, rather than as tools of production. Gen Xers, appreciably more independent than Boomers, are quicker to express their consternation at not being included in decision making that affects them directly.

Providing Xers with flextime and requiring them to ask permission only when it is truly essential for the completion of the task go a long way in affirming their sense of self-worth and respect from the organization (Maynard 1996). Short on patience, Xers demand that those above them let go of the reins as soon as possible. Getting Xers' commitment to the outcome requires that they be able to make a personal impact on that outcome as soon and as much as possible. Getting a degree of commitment to the organization also requires that the system provide them as much control over their work lives as is feasible.

ENRICH THEIR JOBS.
Enrich everybody's job! The early work in job enrichment done by Herzberg (1966), Keith, Robertson & Herzberg (1968), and others laid the groundwork for many of today's larger interventions. Elements of classic job enrichment can be seen in aspects of re-engineering, total quality management, and job redesign. Job enrichment also continues to stand alone as an effective process for increasing motivation.

Again, the only difference between Xer and Boomer responses to chronically dull work is that the Xers will up and leave when it reaches a point of being intolerable. If you want to hang on to the best of the Xers, take a look at what you have them doing and then, where possible, increase the opportunities for

- Achievement

- Recognition for achievement

- Increased responsibility

- Being in a modular work unit or team

- Learning new skills

- Immediate and direct feedback

- Advancement

- Just enjoying the work itself

Retention Factor 3: Growth Opportunities

Hermann (1999) makes the point that the need for continued psychological growth is simply part of the human condition, regardless of generation identity. Sturm (1998) identifies opportunities for personal growth as a key factor in any retention strategy. Boomers and Xers differ in how this need is expressed.

PROMOTE ON THE BASIS OF PERFORMANCE RATHER THAN TENURE.

One of the real bones of contention between the Boomers and the Xers is their respective views about the need to "pay one's dues" (Andrews 1998b). Coolidge (1999) points out that the Xers' biggest complaint about Boomers is that promotions are based on tenure rather than on performance.

Boomers grew up knowing that you had to start at the bottom and then work your way up because, if for no other reason, those who had come before had had to do it also. Whether it was the price of being a tenderfoot in scouting, a pledge in a fraternity, an apprentice in a trade, or just the "new kid on the block," you had to show your worth and recognize the tenure of those who had come before you. This perspective regarding seniority has had several generations over which to become a well-established tenet of organizational life. Probably the best-known examples of this are found in the influence seniority has in union decisions and the role of tenure in academic environments. Generation X represents a major departure from this traditional viewpoint. One pertinent example of this change in thinking is that membership in the Boy Scouts of America, unions, and most Greek letter and other secret societies is at an all-time low.

Xers have little respect for established traditions that are not grounded in present realities. Their position can best be stated as "What's the point of, or the justification for, starting at the bottom when I can already do what's needed now, and as well as anybody else?" The clear demand from the Gen Xers is that promotion be based on one's ability and performance, rather than on one's seniority and political influence. This stance represents the Xers' pragmatic view of organizational life and will have to be respected if you want to keep the best of your new breed.

PROVIDE OPPORTUNITIES FOR TRAINING.

As mentioned earlier, Boomers' expectations were mostly for lifetime employment, whereas most Xers fully anticipate losing at least one job during their working years. Xers also tend to rely much more on themselves than on the organization for their welfare, and are more individualistic than their Boomer counterparts. They welcome anything that will increase their individual capacities to be both more productive and more marketable.

GIVE OPPORTUNITIES FOR OUTSIDE EDUCATION.
Although Xers do not possess that dogged sense of loyalty that keeps them working sixty-hour work weeks indefinitely, they will work long and hard so long as the organization responds to their demand for a more balanced lifestyle. Encouraging learning off the job will probably get a more positive response from this generation than from any that has preceded it.

The nature of today's work requires more education than ever before. When looking at the speed with which technological advances are being made, fighting technical obsolescence is an ongoing battle. Financially supporting advanced degrees, sending people to seminars and workshops, and even giving leaves of absence so that people can go back and concentrate on education are all good means of keeping your people in top-producing condition and with you longer.

Retention Factor 4: Compensation and Rewards

Gen Xers are sometimes described as being highly materialistic. That may or may not be an accurate description, but like everyone else, they have to make a living. Compensation issues are as critical for Xers as they are for Boomers, but how the compensation is delivered is as important a factor as what the compensation is. Following are three suggestions that are geared specifically to Generation X employees.

REWARD INDIVIDUAL AS WELL AS TEAM ACCOMPLISHMENTS.
Generation Xers are both significantly more team-oriented and more highly individualistic than are Baby Boomers. Boomers approach team building as developing a common value system, suborning individual needs to group needs, relying on consensus decision making, and attempting to resolve conflict effectively. The most common motto that captures this mainstream approach to team development is "There is no 'I' in Team."

The Gen X approach to team building is different. It focuses on differentiating members and then finding ways to link them; recognizing that individual needs are often as important as group needs; using any process that gets results; and attempting to manage rather than resolve conflict effectively (Karp 1998).

In order to facilitate the Boomer concept of "we," many systems have done away with rewarding individual accomplishments in favor of rewarding team results. This strategy is founded on the established assumption that what is reinforced will grow and what is not reinforced will wither.

Gen Xers will resist any attempt to merge their individuality into a group identity. While the team concept is important to them, it is not a question of one being sacrificed for the other. Certainly continue with team payoffs, but reinforce individual accomplishments simultaneously. Most important, reward outstanding individual performance even if the team results are not up to the same standard.

USE NONTRADITIONAL BENEFITS.

Gen Xers have a different set of standards about what benefits them than do Baby Boomers. The most valued benefit for Boomers is a good pension plan, whereas the most valued benefit for Xers is good working conditions. The Boomers hold the long view and see a worry-free retirement as the just reward for thirty years of loyal, productive service to one organization. Gen Xers hold the short view, anticipate losing at least one job, and are more concerned about the "here and now" than the "what might be later on." In short, Gen Xers are more interested in making their present life more enjoyable than they are in making their future life more secure.

Merrick (1998) points to a few of the nontraditional benefits that some companies have used to keep Gen X members happy and onboard. SAS Institute threw a World Cup soccer party for people who were at their work stations throughout the championship games. It also has an on-site health care clinic for employees and their families. Life Technologies will send a health aide to an employee's home to care for a sick child. Allied Signal will match donations to employees' favorite charities, up to $1,000. Sun Microsystems provides lactation rooms for new mothers.

The key thing in providing relevant benefits is to remember that what benefits one employee may not be seen as beneficial by another. Survey the younger members of your organization to determine what they want in terms of benefits. While you will still have to provide more traditional benefits to senior members, you can start to tailor what you offer to those younger members whose priorities may be different.

PROVIDE FREQUENT AND VARIED REWARDS.

Boomers, being in for the long haul, have little trouble waiting for pay-offs when they know they are coming. Year-end bonuses and annual performance reviews are part of the traditional corporate culture. Xers have shorter time spans. They require more immediate payoffs and something more than just money. Celebrating at the end of a project, rather than at the end of the fiscal year, is much more important to Xers. The reward at the end of the project immediately reinforces good work and provides closure. Once the present project is over, a younger member is now ready to devote full concentration to new projects coming up.

While Boomers have grown used to large Christmas parties and annual company picnics, Xers prefer more spontaneous work-related social gatherings. They tend to be more appreciative of tickets to a local show or sporting event, an impromptu department beer and pizza party, or a few days off to spend with family or a favorite hobby.

Retention Factor 5: Organizational Culture

Organizations today are much more than income-producing entities. They provide products and services for the community and are the source of growth, personal support, and purpose for their members. Each organization has its own set of identifying values, norms, traditions, and mores. For an organizational culture to be functional, it must also reflect the personalities and values of those people who work in it.

BALANCE WORK AND HOME LIFE.

Whether it's weekends in the laboratory or a seventy-hour week in the law office, a Boomer's worth was often measured by the amount of time he or she was willing to put into the work. Boomers are more process-oriented than Xers, and the way in which they get to a destination is often as important to them as the destination itself.

Gen Xers are far more results-oriented than process-oriented. They are interested in doing what it takes to get the job done rather than in being seen as "hardworking and dedicated." Boomers frequently misinterpret Xers' unwillingness to put in unlimited extended hours on the job as evidence of their being lazy or unmotivated. This is rarely the correct interpretation.

If Xers do not share the Boomers' sense of loyalty and commitment to the organization, they do have a strong commitment to getting the work done right. Xers will work as long and as hard as anyone so long as the demand for grueling hours is seen as a situational necessity and not an organizational value. You will get more mileage, productivity, and appreciation from your Boomers as well if you can unchain them from their desks and convince them that the Xers are right on this one.

Xers draw their identity from many sources outside the workplace. It is therefore very important that Xers have time to enjoy their personal lives. Time for family, friends, hobbies, vacations, travel, more education, and so on, must be not only allowed but encouraged. Xers don't suffer from burnout because they will not allow themselves to become burned out. Most will move on before they let that happen.

CREATE A NONTHREATENING WORK ENVIRONMENT.

Probably the biggest drain on energy and creativity occurs in protecting oneself when self-protection isn't necessary. Corporate life for many Boomers is as much a matter of political survival and forming alliances as it is meeting organizational objectives. Conforming to corporate norms and the dominant culture is a part of the job if you expect to advance, or even survive, in many large organizations. This is what is generally meant by "being a team player."

While this conception is a fact of life for most Boomers, it borders on the unacceptable for most Gen Xers. Xers need to be able to express themselves uniquely and openly, and gain a degree of appreciation for having done so. The safer you make it for people to be more fully who they are and to challenge the status quo in a responsible manner, the more creativity you get. You will be able to keep your best people longer.

Xers won't tolerate threatening work environments as much as their older counterparts. According to Andrews (1999), one critical difference in values between Boomers and Xers is that Boomers tend to punish mistakes whereas Xers tend to reward successes. Reliance on authority, use of organizational rank and status to gain compliance, and threat of disciplinary procedures for nonconforming behaviors are anathema to Xers.

Although performance must be maintained and boundaries must be set on what constitutes inappropriate behavior, how these issues are handled is critical. Allow an employee to see the effect of inappropriate behavior, and make it known that it is the behavior, not the person, that is being addressed.

GRANT FULL ORGANIZATIONAL STATUS.

Just as it is important to promote Gen Xers on the basis of contribution rather than tenure, it is likewise important to grant full organizational status as soon as possible and with the least possible fuss. Xers, as noted earlier, have little respect for organizational tradition and refuse to recognize that they should start at the bottom and pay their dues. The longer you keep them in this stance, the higher the likelihood they are going to be looking for a place where what matters is their ability to contribute, not their age or newness to the organization. Dermody (1998) suggests that accepting trainees into the management culture as quickly as possible is an important retention factor.

Clearly people new to the organization need to be oriented to the culture of the system, meet key people with whom they are going to be working, and know where the cafeteria and the parking lot are. The trick is to accomplish this as quickly and as unobtrusively as possible. The last thing you want to do is parade a newly hired Gen Xer around the organization wearing a pin that says "Junior Assistant Manager Trainee."

Retention Factor 6: Working Relationships with Manager and Co-Workers

One of the more critical factors that distinguishes Boomers from Xers is that the Boomers feel part of the community, whereas Xers feel more isolated. The Xers are the latchkey kids whose moms and dads were both at work when they got home from school. Stereotypically, they tended to associate with a few close friends at the mall and spent the rest of their free time plugged into the computer, the Walkman, or MTV. Their cultural heroes, the ones they could laughingly identify with, were counter-cultural, embodied in such icons as "Beavis and Butthead" and Wayne and Garth in *Wayne's World*. This lifestyle and the conditions that gave birth to it placed a high value on autonomy and independence. It also, simultaneously, created an interpersonal void that places a particularly high need on creating supportive working relationships. The following suggestions relate to working relationships between Gen Xers and their managers.

PROVIDE MENTORING.

The fact that Gen Xers place high value on their individuality suggests they would be receptive to a development strategy that focuses on that characteristic. Providing mentors for the newer members of the organization is one way to customize the skills and perspectives of the mentor to the unique developmental needs of each particular protégé. This not only provides a process for integrating Xers into the system more easily, it has a higher probability of being welcomed by the protégé.

While the key beneficiary of mentoring is the protégé, clear benefits exist for the mentor over and above the warm feelings that come from altruism and an opportunity to leave a "greasy thumb print" on the history of the organization" (Karp 2000). Senior people who willingly take on the job of mentoring Gen Xers are, first of all, people who are not threatened by, or disdainful of, this new group coming in. As they provide information and insights to the Xers about how the system works and how to find a comfortable niche in it, they also gain insights and information about what is important to Gen Xers. The mentors become a conduit for this information for other less-accepting members of the organization, and thereby facilitate the changeover of the organization's culture to become more accommodating of the needs of its younger members.

DO NOT MICRO-MANAGE.

Micro-managing is not a bad thing in itself. The time for effective micro-managing is when the employee is brand new, has no experience in how to do the work correctly, and requires close supervision until he or she can begin to take responsibility for turning out reasonably good results. Micro-managing is best used as a starting point from which one weans the employee into taking full responsibility for his or her output.

Micro-managing under almost any other circumstances is detrimental to the organization's productivity and the employee's growth and development. While just about everyone will resent being inappropriately micro-managed, Xers will let you know of their resentment more loudly and quickly than almost anyone else. Their intolerance for close supervision stems from their independence and need for autonomy as well as from their need to be a participating member of the group.

DEVELOP CLOSER AND MORE SUPPORTIVE RELATIONSHIPS.
One very clear paradox that exists for Generation Xers is their need to be simultaneously fiercely independent and part of a group, with close interpersonal ties. This unique phenomenon calls for a unique managerial approach. The Xers have a strong need to know that they matter, as individuals, to their direct supervisor and to those above them in the system. Effective management requires a closer interpersonal relationship than that requested by those of an earlier generation.

A supervisor should not coddle, patronize, or behave in any way that is inconsistent with his or her specific leadership style. As a matter of fact, any such attempt would probably be quickly rebuffed. Instead, let the Xer know that the supervisor is

- Genuinely concerned about the employee's growth and welfare

- Willing to get to know the employee on more than just a boss-subordinate level

- Inclined to provide more time to interact with the employee over what is narrowly defined by the scope of job demands

The quickest way you can get Gen Xers looking for their next position is to treat them as valued tools of production rather than as people. Gen Xers are intensely loyal to friends rather than to organizations, and tend to establish strong interpersonal ties with those with whom they work. That they are strongly committed to teamwork points to the importance of interpersonal contact on the job. This need goes beyond what is required to complete a project.

As discussed in depth in previous chapters, how teams are structured will have a great deal of impact on how supportive the work environment will be for individual team members. The key points made in our earlier discussion of teams that relate most directly to retaining Gen Xers are the following.

SUPPORT TEAMWORK.

Given that teams already exist, the more a manager can support the concept of a team as a human support system as well as a unit of production, the more responsive the group will be to the needs of its younger members. Gen Xers value both individualism and the need for group process. They require a different team-building paradigm than that which is currently being utilized. Judging from the literature and the current research, the authentic model of team building seems more reflective of Gen X values than does the more traditional model currently in vogue. The challenge lies in accommodating both generational sets of values where there are members of both generations attempting to work collaboratively.

FOSTER INDIVIDUAL RELATIONSHIPS WITHIN THE TEAM.

The two team-building models mentioned above can produce quite different outcomes. Work groups that are developed under authentic values usually result in teams, whereas work groups that are developed purely under the traditional model frequently run the risk of being converted into "love puddles." Since Xers have much stronger loyalties to individuals than to groups, this is probably true as well for their team identities.

Authentic values complement the Gen X value of being much more results-oriented than process-oriented. In authentic teams, it is not so important that everyone like everyone else or see things through the same prism. It's good if we are all in agreement or "singing off the same sheet," but what's important is that we can trust everyone to be honest about what he or she wants and thinks.

Paradoxically, this strategy supports working together because we know that when the work is successfully completed, we can revert back to more natural and comfortable relationships.

PROVIDE OPPORTUNITIES FOR NONWORK ACTIVITIES ON THE JOB SITE.
The work site is the place where most Gen Xers connect socially in terms of meeting the people with whom they have most in common. The more ways you provide for younger organizational members to interact, the higher the probability that important work relationships will be forged as a result. Providing nonwork areas and activities goes a long way toward humanizing the work space and encouraging people to spend a little more time there than they might under other circumstances.

Andrews (1999) points out the value of creating a sense of community in the workplace. Boomers work at work and then go home and work. Xers, on the other hand, work, sleep, eat, and play at work. It's where their friends are. Providing an environment that supports this lifestyle will go a long way in keeping the best of the Xers with you.

Conclusions

Recognizing and responding to change is essential to success in today's organization. The coming of age of Generation X is one of the most significant factors affecting the modern organization. The more quickly key decision makers respond to this reality, the higher the probability that they will be able to provide an environment that will support the needs of the "new breed."

It is important to point out that the youngest members of Generation X are now starting college or joining the workforce. From this point on, the next generation, the "Echo Boomers," will be the ones beginning college or making their entry into the workforce. The clear prediction is that this new generation will be even more grounded in Generation X values than Xers themselves, for three very valid and observable reasons. First, the use of technology is continuing to increase at an astronomic rate as the cost of it is dropping. It is reasonable to expect that shortly every home that has a telephone and TV will also have a computer. Second, there are fewer homes than ever before that have a parent as a full-time custodian, and institutionalized day-care has taken over more and more of the parental role. This results in the probability of the "latchkey syndrome" increasing. Third, the Echo Boomers have little awareness of or personal concern about world conflict outside of what they may pick up watching old World War II movies and the History Channel.

Those conditions that emerged to create the rift between the Boomers and the Xers will continue to be the dominant causal influences of organizational life for some time to come. The paradox is that Boomers, with their long view to organizational survival, are better suited for seeing what's coming. They can make the appropriate changes now to support what can be described as the "Brave New World" just around the corner.

Research Methodology

T his appendix provides technical information about the research back-ground for this book. Two studies were conducted: The first compares team orientation between generations, and the second assesses the level of individualism-collectivism of the two generations.

First Study

In developing our hypothesis for the first study, we used the theoretical work of Goodstein, Cooke, and Goodstein (1987). They discussed two dimensions that are relevant in analyzing team issues: Task Orientation (concern with what the group is working on) and Maintenance Orien-tation (concern for how well the team is working together). Each partic-ipant's values and skills for each of the two dimensions can be measured separately. That is, there is a measure for the extent to which one values task completion and another for the skills one has that are needed to complete the task. There is also a measure of how much one values group maintenance (trust, cohesion, openness) and another of how skilled one is in group maintenance behaviors. Our hypothesis relates to differences between Xers and Baby Boomers on these four variables.

Hypothesis 1: There will be a significant difference between the generations on Task Orientation Skills.

Hypothesis 2: There will be a significant difference between the generations on Task Orientation Values.

Hypothesis 3: There will be a significant difference between the generations on Maintenance Orientation Skills.

Hypothesis 4: There will be a significant difference between the generations on Maintenance Orientation Values.

The samples were obtained by placing a description of the study and its implications on the ODNet listserv on the Internet. The total sample was from six organizations: three high-tech firms, one financial company, a government agency, and students from a state university. The student sample was taken from the university courses that both investigators were conducting at the time. This was done to provide a sample that was all Generation X and that had not been subject to the corporate or large-system values and culture. Table 4 describes the characteristics of the total sample, which consisted of 398 participants.

The instrument used was the *Team Orientation Behavior Inventory* (TOBI), developed by Goodstein et al. (1987). The TOBI is composed of 56 items and measures four variables: task skills, task values, maintenance skills, and maintenance values. The TOBI reports the following reliability alpha coefficients:

Task Orientation		*Maintenance Orientation*		
Values	= 0.74	Values	=	0.81
Skills	= 0.79	Skills	=	0.83

Validity was established using independent observers. For a detailed explanation of the TOBI, see Goodstein et al. (1987).

In addition to using the TOBI, data were collected in several demographic characteristics of the sample. A biographic inventory was constructed to get salient characteristics of the total population and of each separate sample. It was important to obtain data for each of the contributing samples given the possibility that organizational and demographic variables might have as much effect on results as societal variables.

TABLE 4 *Demographic Characteristics of the Total Sample (First Study)*

VARIABLE	MEAN	S.D.	N	PERCENTAGE
Age	34.97	9.30	398	100.00
Baby Boomers	43.41	4.89	189	47.49
Generation Xers	27.33	4.47	209	52.51
Gender				
Male			184	46.9
Female			208	53.1
Current Position				
Salary/Hourly employee			241	61.3
Supervisor			22	5.6
Manager			30	7.6
Other			100	25.4
Highest Level of Education				
Less than high school			1	0.3
High school			82	20.7
Two years of college			191	48.1
Bachelor's degree			97	24.4

Means and standard deviations were calculated for each of the four dependent variables under each age group (Baby Boomers and Generation Xers). The objective was to see the direction of the difference between means. Table 5 shows the mean for each dependent variable under each age group. A relatively larger difference was observed for maintenance values. The maintenance value mean for Generation Xers is higher than the Boomers', indicating that Generation X subjects may have a statistically higher value for teamwork.

Because the dependent variable is a vector of highly correlated elements, multivariate analysis is appropriate (Hair et al., 1979). Table 6 shows the Pearson correlation scores among the four dependent

TABLE 5 *Descriptive Statistics for the Dependent Variables*

VARIABLE	MEAN	S.D.	N
Maintenance Skills			
Baby Boomers	72.08	11.18	189
Generation Xers	72.42	10.82	209
Maintenance Values			
Baby Boomers	72.95	8.24	189
Generation Xers	75.28	7.66	209
Task Skills			
Baby Boomers	70.19	13.18	189
Generation Xers	70.89	12.53	209
Task Values			
Baby Boomers	73.96	9.15	189
Generation Xers	75.27	9.78	209

TABLE 6 *Scale Reliability and Correlation for Dependent Variables*

VARIABLE	1	2	3	4
Maintenance Skills	(0.82)			
Maintenance Values	0.479**	(0.61)		
Task Skills	0.775**	0.316**	(0.80)	
Task Values	0.419	0.591**	0.357**	(0.61)

ªScale reliability is in parentheses on the diagonal.
** p < 0.01

variables as well as the reliability of each measurement. A multivariate analysis of covariance (MANCOVA) was performed to test the effect of age group on all dependent variables simultaneously. Four control variables (gender, organization, highest level of education, and current position) were included to determine the effect of age group after other variables that may influence the dependent variable scores are accounted

TABLE 7 *Analysis of Covariance*

	MAINTENANCE SKILLS	MAINTENANCE VALUES	TASK SKILLS	TASK VALUES
Main Factor				
Age group	0.015	6.385*	0.004	0.291
Covariates				
Gender	0.17	11.512**	1.403	3.793
Highest level of education	10.409**	0.344	25.521**	0.001
Organization	8.932**	2.833	9.043**	9.178**
Current position	2.717	.232	5.906**	1.024

* $p < 0.05$
** $p < 0.01$

for. Finally, analysis of covariance (ANCOVA) was performed to test the effects of age group on each dependent variable after removing the effect of the control variables.

A MANCOVA procedure, which was used to test the overall effect of the age group after the effects of several covariates were removed, yielded a significant result (Wilks' Lambda = 0.972, F = 2.448, p = 0.046). This means that at least one of the mean differences is significantly different from zero. Individual analysis of covariance was performed to test each mean difference. Results are presented in table 7.

Table 7 indicates that there is a significant difference between age groups on their maintenance value score mean. This result supports hypothesis 4. No statistical difference was found on the other dependent variables.

Second Study

One common thread in the literature is that Generation Xers are considered to be highly individualistic people, and it would seem that this characteristic might block a smooth process in a team setting. Therefore, the second study was conducted to measure levels of individualism in the two generations. The *Individualism-Collectivism Scales* (ICS) instrument, consisting of 20 items (Wagner 1995), was chosen for this study. The ICS instrument measures five independent variables: self-reliance, competitiveness, solitary work preference, supremacy of group interests, and supremacy of group goals. Items in the instrument are shown in table 8. For more details, see Ramamoorthy & Carroll (1998). In addition to the ICS, demographic variables were collected similar to those used in the first study.

Our hypothesis was that Generation Xers would be significantly more individualistic than Baby Boomers across the five variables as measured by the ICS instrument.

Hypothesis 1: Generation Xers will be significantly more self-reliant than Boomers.

Hypothesis 2: Generation Xers will be significantly more competitive than Boomers.

Hypothesis 3: Generation Xers will prefer to work solitarily significantly more than Boomers.

Hypothesis 4: Boomers are more prone to sacrificing personal pursuits than Generation Xers.

Hypothesis 5: Generation Xers will perceive that enlightened self-interest is a positive force for group productivity significantly more than Boomers.

The total sample for the second study included eight organizations. Table 9 describes the characteristics of the total sample. The number of surveys totaled 500, but only the 437 that were Baby Boomers and Generation Xers were part of the analysis.

A factor analysis was performed to verify that items loaded in the expected factors. The results confirmed the literature findings, and items loaded as expected: items 1 through 5 (see table 9) loaded together to form the factor self-reliance; items 6 through 10 measure the level of competitiveness; items 11 through 13 quantify solitary work preference; items 14 through 17 measure supremacy of group interest; and items 16 through 20 measure supremacy of group goals. Of special interest for this research was the last factor because it reveals a different point of view about what conditions are needed to have a good team, which is

TABLE 8 *Items in the Individualism–Collectivism Instrument*

1. Only those who depend on themselves get ahead in life.

2. To be superior, a person must stand alone.

3. If you want something done right, you've got to do it yourself.

4. What happens to me is my own doing.

5. In the long run, the only person you can count on is yourself.

6. Winning is everything.

7. I feel that winning is important in both work and games.

8. Success is the most important thing in life.

9. It annoys me when other people perform better than I do.

10. Doing your best isn't enough: it is important to win.

11. I prefer to work with others in a group rather than working alone.

12. Given the choice, I would rather do a job where I can work alone rather than doing a job where I have to work with others in a group.

13. Working with a group is better than working alone.

14. People should be made aware that if they are going to be part of a group then they are sometimes going to have to do things they don't want to do.

15. People who belong to a group should realize that they're not always going to get what they personally want.

16. People in a group should realize that they sometimes are going to have to make sacrifices for the sake of the group as a whole.

17. People in a group should be willing to make sacrifices for the sake of the group's well-being.

18. A group is more productive when its members do what they want to do rather than what the group wants them to do.

19. A group is most efficient when its members do what they think is best rather than doing what the group wants them to do.

20. A group is more productive when its members follow their own interests and concerns.

that people with individualistic tendencies would be more likely to take care of their personal concerns first as a prerequisite to a highly effective team.

Following the factor analysis, factor scores were calculated and analyzed to see the direction of the difference. In all cases, Generation Xers obtained average factor scores indicating higher levels of individualism than those of Baby Boomers.

The next step was to use factor scores to perform individual analysis of covariance using four variables as covariates: organization where the subject works, highest level of education, gender, and current position. The analysis compares Baby Boomers with Generation Xers along the five variables measured in the individualism-collectivism instrument. The results are shown in table 10. The analysis indicated that two factors are statistically significant: self-reliance and enlightened self-interest, which are related to hypotheses 1 and 5. This supports the hypothesis that, at least in two specific variables, Generation Xers are significantly more individualistic than Baby Boomers.

TABLE 9 *Demographic Characteristics of the Total Sample (Second Study)*

VARIABLE	MEAN	S.D.	N	PERCENTAGE
Age	40.25	12.64	500*	100.00
Baby Boomers	46.81	4.68	230	52.63
Generation Xers	27.15	4.99	207	47.37
Gender				
Male			306	61.7
Female			190	38.3
Current Position				
Salary/Hourly employee			193	38.4
Supervisor			132	26.2
Manager			83	16.5
Other			88	17.5
Highest Level of Education				
Less than high school			2	0.4
High school			45	8.9
Two years of college			161	32.0
Bachelor's degree			245	48.7
Advanced degree			44	8.7

* This includes everyone in the sample including subjects who are neither Generation Xers nor Baby Boomers.

TABLE 10 *Analysis of Covariance for Individualism-Collectivism Factor Scores*

	FACTOR 1[1]	FACTOR 2	FACTOR 3	FACTOR 4	FACTOR 5
Main Factor					
Age group	15.994**	1.364	.147	.168	4.213*
Covariates					
Gender	1.973	23.101**	7.941**	2.616	4.545*
Highest level of education	.131	.814	8.850**	.244	.017
Organization	6.245**	.833	1.193	.121	3.472
Current position	2.732	.717	1.730	.134	8.470**

[1]Factor 1: Self-reliance, Factor 2: Competitiveness, Factor 3: Solitary work preference, Factor 4: Supremacy of group interests, and Factor 5: Supremacy of group goals.
* $p < 0.05$
** $p < 0.01$

Team Development Timeline

*T*he Team Development Timeline is a comprehensive overview of characteristics of each phase of a team's development, as well as the behavioral indicators that a team is beginning to transition from one phase to the next.

For each phase, general characteristics are noted, along with the team's developmental needs and techniques to support that development. The roles of the coach, the facilitator, and the individual team member are also defined in terms of what each should be doing to help the team successfully navigate the phase. As the team masters each phase, members will begin to display new behaviors that herald the team's passage into the next phase. The behaviors that typify each transition period are described so that they may be recognized as hallmarks of transition rather than indications of decline, as they are often mistaken to be.

The Team Development Timeline is not intended to be a cook book for authentic teams. Rather, it is a framework within which authentic teams can take root and thrive.

Team Development Timeline—Phase 1

CHARACTERISTICS	DEVELOPMENT NEEDS	SUPPORTING TECHNIQUES	COACH'S ROLE: TEACHING	FACILITATOR'S ROLE: STRUCTURE	TEAM MEMBER'S ROLE: LEARNING
Team members are polite to one another; minimal conflict.	Structure for operation as a team: what to do and how to do it.	Hold regular meetings with defined start and stop times; practice good meetings.	Help the team develop a clear mission/charter.	Provide structure and direction to the team.	Attend team meetings and team training sessions.
Difficult for team to prioritize activities.	Focus on goals; clear understanding of how goals affect the organization's performance	Flowcharts of work processes; awareness of internal and external customers.	Facilitate areas of conflict between team and others of the organization.	Push responsibility down to the team while maintaining high standard of team operation.	Participate in team discussions; practice new skills.
Team activities are seen as in addition to the "real" job.	Integrating team activities into the "real" job.	Establish guidelines for how the team will work together.	Hold team accountable for meeting task and process goals.	Ensure specific goals and measurement methods are in place.	Participate in team discussions; practice new skills.

Team Development Timeline—Phase 1 into Phase 2

The team is moving into the next stage when

- Attendance at meetings drops off; people come late; assignments are not completed.
- Individual goals and issues start to become evident and are more important than team goals.
- Cliques or subgroups form.
- The coach and/or facilitator is frequently challenged.
- High levels of frustration are evident for coach and team members.
- "What's in it for me?" is a frequently asked question.
- Louder, more frequent complaints about team meetings are heard.
- Members are more willing to take personal risk, disagree with the norm.

To help the team move forward

- Reflect decisions back to the team; ask, "How would you handle it?"
- Support the group as it attempts to work through problems; do not give easy answers, but do give lots of structure.
- Split subgroups whenever possible: put them on separate task forces, rearrange seats in meetings so they are not seated together, give assignments (such as being the scribe) that require attention be paid to the discussion.
- Address personal conflicts by meeting with the individuals involved, both or all at the same time, to discuss their disagreements and work on mutually agreeable solutions.
- Redirect personal conflict to focus on the issue or the impact on getting the work done.
- Challenge team members by playing devil's advocate and/or by representing the minority view in discussions.
- Encourage members to talk about their frustrations with the team and what it would take for the team to be successful.
- Confront problem areas with the team; don't let team members avoid critical issues or disagreements.
- Ensure that all team members receive training.
- Model behaviors you would like to see team members use with one another, especially listening skills and respect for differences.

Team Development Timeline—Phase 2

CHARACTERISTICS	DEVELOPMENT NEEDS	SUPPORTING TECHNIQUES	COACH'S ROLE: TEACHING	FACILITATOR'S ROLE: STRUCTURE	TEAM MEMBER'S ROLE: LEARNING
High relationship tension; individual characteristics become sources of irritation.	Conflict management skills; understanding positive aspects of conflict.	Training in mixed groups (not as intact teams); individual application to own team situation.	Actively counsel and support the facilitator; help prep for and debrief after each meeting.	Hold the team accountable for its own success; remind the team of its guidelines.	Bring issues and concerns to the team during meetings.
High task tension; energy is being drained by the conflict; job is not getting done.	Problem-solving and/or project management skills; structure.	Training as an intact team, with application to real team issues.	Hold the team accountable for performance; maintain standards.	Provide structure for difficult tasks and interactions; listen/test for common ground.	Honestly agree or disagree with the issues.
Hidden agendas emerge.	Consensus decision-making skills.	Training as an intact team, with application to real team issues.	Model good listening skills; hear all sides.	Continue to hold all meetings; stick to the agenda.	Accept accountability for issues that belong to the team.
Power struggles are evident; definite win-lose mentality. Subgroups are powerful. There is little cooperation and less collaboration.	Options for decision making; clearly understood consequences of behavior as determined by the team.	Confront the team with consequences of its own decision-making difficulties, i.e., inability to reach higher levels of maturity.	Hold the team to its own guidelines; change guidelines only if warranted and team agrees.	Review processes learned in training; apply known skills to conflict situations; hold team accountable for its own behavior.	Use skills learned previously; accept ownership of team's success.
Frustration and disappointment for all involved.	Understanding of group process; structure and models; strong leadership.	Agenda items that encourage team discussions about what is happening to the team (process).	Be patient; allow the team to learn how to resolve and be responsible for its own issues.	Push issues back to the team for resolution; do not allow the team to hold you responsible for its problems.	Think through decisions and accept accountability for outcomes.

Team Development Timeline–Phase 2 into Phase 3

The team is moving into the next stage when

- Individual team members begin to suggest ways of getting the assignment back on track.
- There is agreement to disagree; expectations that there should be no conflict or that conflict cannot be overcome give way to thoughts of managing the conflict and moving beyond it.
- Conflict is positioned differently: Individuals make "I" statements instead of speaking as if for the group.
- Team members begin to look for things they agree on.
- Frustration turns into action: commitment to the team's task emerges as individual goals are put aside or integrated into the team's goals.
- Some team members may leave the team; those who stay are ready to try to make it work.

To help the team move forward

- Make it clear to the team that the management of the company is committed to the team structures.
- Solicit ideas from the team about how to make things more effective in the future.
- Encourage the team to review its guidelines and to revise them if necessary.
- Allow the team to redesign itself in order to make things work, if redesign is a step the team feels is necessary.
- Expand boundaries as the team proves its ability to address more difficult issues and decisions.
- Make suggestions to the team for ways to improve; position suggestions as your ideas and equal to those offered by team members.
- Accept that some people will never work well on a team. Work with them and the team to identify an appropriate role for them to play as an individual contributor, or help them find another position within the company that is better suited to their style.
- Revisit training done in earlier stages because it will have a completely different meaning at this point than it did before.
- Identify and congratulate the team on genuine success; never take for granted that the team will recognize its own success.

Team Development Timeline—Phase 3

CHARACTERISTICS	DEVELOPMENT NEEDS	SUPPORTING TECHNIQUES	COACH'S ROLE: TEACHING	FACILITATOR'S ROLE: STRUCTURE	TEAM MEMBER'S ROLE: LEARNING
Established and understood goals, standards of performance and measurement.	Information, information, information!	Methods for tracking performance; access to necessary information.	Liaison with other parts of the organization to ensure access to information.	Hold team meetings to an agreed process; lead team in measuring progress against goals.	Be open and honest with other team members.
Shared responsibility; no finger-pointing	Equally informed on all issues affecting the team.	Team-building activities and/or exercises.	Serve as an "expert resource."	Rotate role.	Share in rotation of roles.
Standardized procedures for routine tasks.	Process flowcharts; ability to streamline when appropriate.	Cross-training.	Be available to support and advise as appropriate.	Lead the group in process checks.	Help maintain team effectiveness.
Division of work managed within the team; match talents with tasks.	Understanding of workloads and individual capabilities.	Expanded boundaries and opportunities to learn new skills.	Continue to monitor boundaries; expand as appropriate.	Hold team accountable to its own guidelines and mission.	Help establish and abide by guidelines set by the team.
Confidence in team's abilities; willingness to call in expertise if it is not in the team.	Advanced training in interpersonal skills and in task activities.	Regular training events designed to enhance team effectiveness.	Model behaviors desired of team members.	Function as a team member; offer input when you have it.	Facilitate if the designated facilitator wants to participate in the discussion.
Desire to know more about and interact with other teams.	Understanding of how team interfaces with other teams.	Cross-team opportunities.	Encourage and foster cross-team interactions.	Clarify structure for cross-team activities.	Be willing to visit other teams and/or represent your team.
See Coach as an "expert resource," not a supervisor.	Coach as teacher and facilitator.	Role flexibility; members take turns filling various roles.	Support and teach; facilitate, but don't dominate.	Facilitate equal exchange of information.	Look to team for resolution of issues, not to coach.

Team Development Timeline—Phase 3 into Phase 4

The team is moving into the next stage when

- Team members uniformly understand goals and how performance will be measured.
- There is equal participation in meetings; assignments are done on time; discussions are open.
- There is fast and efficient handling of routine tasks.
- Group norms are understood.
- The coach is treated as an equal team member; his or her opinion is subject to challenge, just as that of any other team member.
- Team members acknowledge and often refer to strengths of other team members.
- There is a willingness to take on tasks as developmental opportunities and to build strength in a current area of weakness.
- Team members help one another develop their skills/talents.
- Any team member may seek out required resources; no longer just the coach's role.
- The team may seek feedback from those outside the team.
- Team members identify themselves as part of the team.

To help the team move forward

- Give the team members increasing levels of responsibility and accountability. Monitor their progress: If they fail, help them learn from the experience. If they succeed, celebrate with them.
- Offer your opinions as an equal; accept that there may be better ideas from others.
- Share your team's successes with others; allow others to benefit from what your team has learned.
- Encourage members of your team to serve as mentors to other teams.
- Watch for signs of groupthink and take appropriate steps to eliminate it.
- Encourage the rotation of team members into other teams to enhance the effectiveness of all teams.
- Encourage the rotation of new team members into this team to keep ideas fresh and to foster growth.
- Encourage the rotation of roles within the team on a regular, pre-set schedule.
- Encourage regular checks of how the team is working together (process).
- Encourage regular team-building events.

Team Development Timeline–Phase 4

CHARACTERISTICS	DEVELOPMENT NEEDS	SUPPORTING TECHNIQUES	COACH'S ROLE: TEACHING	FACILITATOR'S ROLE: STRUCTURE	TEAM MEMBER'S ROLE: LEARNING
Guidelines are observed in all team interactions.	Periodic check to see if guidelines are still appropriate; revisions as required.	Flexibility in guidelines; confidence that all will observe agreed-on guidelines.	Serve as an "expert resource" to the team.	Continue to guide the team according to its agreed-on processes for interaction.	View all team activities as part of the job.
Task skills are routinely updated; there is continuous improvement of work processes.	Cross-training; skill training/enhancement	Allow the team to design and implement training as it sees fit.	Provide information about organizational issues that may affect the team.	Be sure someone is keeping track of team member training.	Seek additional training to meet performance standards.
Shared leadership; communication is open and direct; mutual influence is evident.	Feedback on leadership performance.	Team member gives feedback on how members are filling their assigned roles.	Monitor, advise, and support the team as needed.	Abide by guidelines for effective meetings.	Abide by standards of performance set by the team.
Innovation and risk taking are supported within the team.	Increased opportunities to create visions of the future.	Facilitated sessions devoted to creating a vision for the team and/or the company.	Provide strategic insights and perspectives.	Bring in an outside facilitator for special sessions; serve as a participating team member.	Engage in outside-the-box thinking; use skills and abilities to project future activities.
Roles and responsibilities are defined, clearly understood, and shared.	Charter and guidelines for roles that are critical for team success.	Flexibility to create appropriate roles to fill team needs.	Ensure that those who are in team roles are equipped to fill them properly.	Observe rotation schedules; add to agenda when appropriate.	Serve in roles as required to support shared accountability.
Team decisions are quick and sound.	Develop clear rationale for decisions.	Full consideration given to team recommendations and actions.	If a team decision cannot be supported, explain why and help the team learn from it.	Facilitate effective and efficient team meetings, using skills as required.	Accept feedback about decisions that are not accepted.

Team Development Timeline–Phase 4 into High Performance

The team has achieved high performance when

- Team members are aligned on purpose.
- Team's focus is on task and results; "process" has become a natural rhythm for the team.
- There is shared responsibility for a wide variety of decisions.
- Communication is at a high level, both within the team and with those outside of the team.
- Team members seek and respond to feedback.
- Team members quickly respond to issues affecting the team and/or achievement of its goals.
- There is ongoing discovery of creative talents within the team.
- Team members are willing to accept calculated risks that help the team achieve its goals.
- Synergy is visible to all who observe the team in action.
- Team members are aligned on values and commitment.
- New team members are quickly assimilated into the team.

To help the team maintain high performance

- Encourage time for team-building activities on a regular basis.
- Ensure time for continued development of team member skills.
- Expand team boundaries as appropriate.
- Allow team input into membership changes.
- Review team decisions and actions to ensure compliance with organizational goals and values.
- Monitor for groupthink and call attention to any symptoms.
- Provide regular feedback based on personal observations of the team at work.
- Support and interact with team members individually as well as collectively.

References

Andrews, J. (1998a, March–April). Recruitment: Cultivate potential, reward results. *Credit Union Executive, 38*(2), 30–33.

Andrews, J. (1998b, July–August). Retaining the Generation X workforce. *Credit Union Executive, 38*(4), 40–42.

Blake, R., and Mouton, J. (1964). *The managerial grid.* Houston, TX: Gulf.

Bliss and Associates. (1999). Cost of turnover spreadsheet. Bliss Report, Wayne, NJ.

Cattell, R. B. (1957). *Personality and motivation structure and measurement.* New York: World Book.

Coolidge, S. D. (1999, August 9). Work and money: Generations apart. *Christian Science Monitor*, pp. 11–14

Dermody, M. B. (1998, December). Recruitment and retention of managers: Developing a management-career package. *Cornell Hotel & Restaurant Administration Quarterly, 39*(6), 20–25.

Dettmer, W. (1997). *Goldratt's theory of constraints: A system approach to continuous improvement.* Milwaukee, WI: ASQC Quality Press.

Flynn, G. (1996, November). Xers vs. teamwork. *Personnel Journal, 75*(11), 86–89.

Goldratt, E. (1994). *It's not luck.* Great Barrington, MA: North River Press.

Goodstein, L. D., Cooke, P., and Goodstein, J. (1994). In J. W. Pfeiffer (ed.), *The team orientation and behavior inventory* (pp. 173–186). San Diego, CA: Pfeiffer.

Hair, J. F., Jr., Anderson, R. E., Tatham, R. L., and Grablowsky, B. J. (1979). *Multivariate data analysis.* Tulsa, OK: Petroleum Publishing.

Herman, S. (1974). The shadow of organization development. In J. Pfeiffer and J. Jones (eds.), *The 1974 annual handbook for group facilitators.* San Diego, CA: Pfeiffer.

Herman, S., and Kornich, M. (1977). *Authentic management: A gestalt orientation to organizations and their development.* Reading, MA: Addison-Wesley.

Hersey, P., and Blanchard, K. H. (1969). *Management of organizational behavior: Utilizing human resources.* Englewood Cliffs, NJ: Prentice-Hall.

Herzberg, F. (1968). One more time: How do you motivate your employees? *Harvard Business Review 46*(1), 53–62.

Herzberg, F. (1959). *Work and the nature of man.* Cleveland, OH: World Press.

Holtz, G. T. (1995). *Welcome to the jungle: The why behind Generation X.* New York: St. Martin's Press.

Jaffe, J., Hunter, W., Katz, M., and Taylor, D. L. (1996). Senior market offers growing opportunities. *Best's Review,* Life–Health Insurance Edition, *96*(10), 76.

Karp, H. B. (2000). A pragmatic primer for mentoring. *The 2000 annual, Vol. 1, Consulting* (pp. 201–211). San Francisco: Jossey-Bass/Pfeiffer.

Karp, H. B. (1998). Conventional human resource development and the gestalt approach. *The 1998 annual, Vol. 2, Consulting.* San Francisco: Jossey-Bass/Pfeiffer.

Karp, H. B. (1995). *Personal power: An unorthodox guide to success.* Lake Worth, FL: Gardner Press.

Likert, R. (1961). *New patterns of management.* New York: McGraw-Hill.

Loysk, R. (1997, March–April). How to manage an Xer. *Futurist 31*(2), 41.

Mahedy, W., and Bernardi, J. (1994). *A generation alone.* Downers Grove, IL: InterVarsity Press.

Massey, M. (1986). *The Massey triad program 2: What you are is not what you have to be* (Video). (Available from Enterprise Media LLC, 91 Harvey Street, Cambridge, MA 02140.)

Maynard, R. (1996, November). A less stressed workforce: Managing Generation X employees. *Nation's Business 84*(11), 50.

Mayo, E. (1919). *Democracy and freedom: An essay in social logic.* Melbourne, Australia: McMillan.

McGregor, D. (1957, November). The human side of enterprise. *Management Review,* p. 26.

Merrick, A. (1998, September). Companies go the extra mile to retain employees. *R & D, 40*(10), 3–4.

Muchnick, M. (1996). *Naked management: Bare essentials for motivating the X-Generation at work.* Boca Raton, FL: St. Lucie Press.

Myers, I. B. (1998). *Introduction to Type®.* (6th ed.). Palo Alto, CA: Consulting Psychologists Press, Inc.

Paul, W., Robertson, K., and Herzberg, F. (1969) Job enrichment pays off. *Harvard Business Review, 47*(2), 61–78.

Perls, F. (1973). *The gestalt approach and eye witness to therapy.* Ben Lomond, CA: Science and Behavior Books.

Ramamoorthy, N., and Carroll, S. J. (1998). Individualism/collectivism orientations and reactions toward alternative human resource management practices. *Human Relations, 51*(5), 571–588.

Roethisberger, F. J., and Dickson, W. J. (1936). *Management and the worker.* Cambridge, MA: Harvard University Press.

Seabrook, J. (1997, August 18) Tackling the competition. *New Yorker, 23*(24), 42–51.

Smith, J. (1999, July 3). The deep dive. *Nightline.* Tom Bettag, producer. ABC Transcript #4728.

Sturm, D. (1998, September). Five ingredients for an employee retention formula. *HR Focus, 75*(9), 9.

Tannenbaum, R., and Schmidt, W. H. (1958, March–April). How to choose a leadership pattern. *Harvard Business Review, 36*, 95–101.

Taylor, F. W. (1911). *Scientific management.* New York: Harper.

Tuckman, B. W. (1965). Developmental sequence in small groups. *Psychological Bulletin, 63*(6), 384–399.

Tulgen, B. (1995). *Managing Generation X.* Santa Monica, CA: Merritt.

Wagner, J., III. (1995). Studies of individualism-collectivism: Effects on cooperation in groups. *Academy of Management Review 38*(1), 152–172.

Woker, C. (1999, July). Luring Generation X with opportunity instead of stability. *New Steel, 15*(7), 60.

Yablonka, E. (1999, April). IT staffing: Retention is cheaper than recruiting. *Health Management Technology, 20*(3), 32–34.

Index

adversary relationship: avoidance of, 118–120; breaking of, 116; case study example of, 124–125; changing of, 120–121; characteristics of, 116–118; concepts of, 115–116; conflict in, 116–118; contract, 127–128; damage caused by, 116; dehumanizing effects, 119–120; facilitator for mediating, 122–123; generation conflict and, 118; halting of, 120–131; naturalness of, 115–116; pain transfer in, 121–122, 124; positions of individuals in, 123–124; redefining of roles in, 125–127; techniques for resolving, 128–130

authentic teams: academic model of, 48–49; autonomy, 40, 58; building of, 51–74; case study example of, 72–73; cohesion of, 70; conflict, 40, 42, 59; coordinator of. *See* coach; daily structure integrated into operational structure, 69–70; description of, 95; environment created by, 52, 71; forming stage of, 55–59, 164–165; Gestalt psychology influences, 37–39; goals of, 97–98; high-performance. *See* high-performing teams; individual identity valued in, 42; members of. *See* team members; model of, 54; norming stage of, 68–71, 168–169; obstacles to achieving goal of, 97–99; origins of, 37; performing stage of, 71–74, 170–171; problem-

solving approach, 95–112; revisiting of guidelines by, 70; rewarding of, 75–76, 119; self-empowerment, 43; storming stage of, 59–68, 166–167; supporting of. *See* supporting of authentic teams; team-building approach, 45–46; team leader/coach's role in, 43–44; Theory of Constraints approach. *See* Theory of Constraints; traditional team vs., 39–44, 68; working relationship as viewed by, 41

authority, lack of respect for: by Baby Boomers, 15, 24, 76; by Generation Xers, 23

authority role: Baby Boomers in, 23–24; decision making, 79; Generation Xers in, 23–24; subordinates, 78

autonomy, 40, 58, 71

Baby Boomers: characteristics of, 2, 8–9, 31–32, 131, 134–136; decision-making approach, 19–20; definition of, 2, 7; evolution of, 14–16; family influences, 17; group identity valued by, 50; increases in, 8, 134; influences on, 8–9; integration with Generation Xers. *See* integration; job security concerns, 20; labor force predominance by, 12; loyalty of, 20, 50; military influences, 14–15; outlook of, 5; perception of, 32; population growth of, 8, 134; power

traditional team *(continued)*
team-building approach, 44,
114; team leader/coach's role in,
43–44; working relationship
as viewed by, 41
traditions, 141
training opportunities, 141–142
turnover, employee: costs of, 134;
description of, 11; productivity
effects, 11; team performance
effects, 82–85

values: of Baby Boomers, 5; of Generation Xers, 5, 22; traditional
team, 37
Vietnam War, 14–15

work: content of, 138–140; fun in,
139; home life balanced with,
144–145
work environment: authentic team
effects, 52, 71; casual attire in,
137; community sense culti-
vated in, 150; effect on employee retention, 137–138; nonthreatening, 145–146; nonwork
activities offered in, 150
work ethic: Baby Boomer, 9–10;
Generation Xer, 10
workspace: personalization of, 138;
privacy in, 137

Xers. *See* Generation Xers